LOVE, SEX & GOD

Bill Ameiss and Jane Graver

For ages
14 to
young adult
and parents

This second edition was formerly titled *Lord of Life,*
Lord of Me in the Concordia Sex Education Series
published in 1982.

Book Five of the Learning about Sex Series

The titles in the series:

Book 1: Why Boys and Girls Are Different
Book 2: Where Do Babies Come From?
Book 3: How You Are Changing
Book 4: Sex and the New You
Book 5: Love, Sex, and God
Book 6: How to Talk Confidently
with Your Child about Sex

Developed under the auspices of the Family Life Department
Board for Parish Services
The Lutheran Church—Missouri Synod

Scripture quotations marked TEV are from the Good News Bible, the Bible in TO-
DAY'S ENGLISH VERSION. Copyright © American Bible Society 1966, 1971,
1976. Used by permission.

Scripture quotations marked Phillips are from J. B. Phillips: THE NEW TESTA-
MENT IN MODERN ENGLISH, Revised Edition © J. B. Phillips 1958, 1960, 1972.
Used by permission of Macmillian Publishing Company.

Illustrations by Maritz Communications Company. 1988 cover design by Concordia
Publishing House.

Copyright © 1982, 1988
Concordia Publishing House
3558 South Jefferson Avenue
Saint Louis, Missouri 63118

MANUFACTURED IN THE UNITED STATES OF AMERICA

1 2 3 4 5 6 7 8 9 10   97 96 95 94 93 92 91 90 89 88

Contents

Editor's Foreword

This book is one of a series of six published under the auspices of the Board for Parish Services of The Lutheran Church—Missouri Synod through its family life department.

Originally published in 1982, the series was updated in 1988. To indicate more precisely that it's a *sex*-education series, all books were given new titles and cover designs. Books four through six were expanded to include topics of current concern such as the sexually transmitted diseases AIDS and chlamydia.

Books in the series are (former titles in parentheses): *Why Boys and Girls Are Different* (*Each One Specially*) (Ages 3–5); *Where Do Babies Come From?* (*I Wonder Why*) (Ages 6–8); *How You Are Changing* (*How You Got to Be You*) (Ages 8–11); *Sex and the New You* (*The New You*) (Ages 11–14); *Love, Sex, and God* (*Lord of Life, Lord of Me*) (Age 14 +); and *How to Talk Confidently with Your Child about Sex* (*Sexuality: God's Precious Gift to Parents and Children*).

The last book in the series is designed for adults, to help them deal with their own sexuality, as well as provide practical assistance for married and single parents in their role as sex educators in the home.

Love, Sex, and God is the fifth book in the series. It is written especially for youth ages 14 and older—and, of course, for the parents, teachers, and other significant grownups who may want to discuss the book with them.

Like its predecessor, the new *Learning about Sex* series provides information about the social-psychological and physiological aspects of human sexuality. But more: it does so from a distinctively Christian point of view, in the context of our relationship to the God who created us and redeemed us in Jesus Christ.

The series presents sex as another good gift from God which is to be used responsibly.

Each book in the series is graded—in vocabulary and in the amount of information it provides. It answers the questions that persons at each age level typically ask.

Because children vary widely in their growth rates and interest levels, parents and other concerned adults will want to preview each book in the series, directing the child to the next graded book when he or she is ready for it.

In addition to reading each book, you can use them as starting points for casual conversation and when answering other questions a child might have.

This book can also be used as a mini-unit or as part of another course of study in a Christian school setting. (Correlated video resources are available for both curricular and home use.) Whenever the book is used in a class setting, it's important to let the parents know beforehand, since they have the prime responsibility for the sex education of their children.

While parents will appreciate the help of the school, they will want to know what is being taught. As the Christian home and the Christian school work together, Christian values in sex education can be more effectively strengthened.

Frederick J. Hofmeister, M.D., FACOG, Wauwatosa, Wisconsin, served as medical adviser for the series. Rev. Ronald W. Brusius, secretary of family life education, Board for Parish Services, served as chief subject matter consultant.

In addition to the staffs of the Board for Parish Services and Concordia Publishing House, the following special consultants helped conceptualize the series: Darlene Armbruster, board member, National Lutheran Parent-Teacher League; Betty Brusius, executive director, National Lutheran Parent-Teacher League; Margaret Gaulke, elementary school guidance counselor; Priscilla Henkelman, early childhood specialist; Rev. Lee Hovel, youth specialist; Robert G. Miles, Lutheran Child and Family Service of Michigan; Margaret Noettl, family life specialist; and Rev. Prof. Rex Spicer, D.Min., family life consultant.

Rev. Earl H. Gaulke, Ph.D.

Introduction

What do other people really think of me?
Am I normal?
How can I let him know I like him a lot?
How can I get to know her better?
How far is it OK to go with my steady?
How can I tell if I'm really in love?
What if I'm in deep trouble?
Where should I go for help?

These are not unusual questions. The purpose of this book is to explore them and a whole range of related questions and subjects. We'll draw on the questions, struggles, and experiences of many young people as they too have faced the responsibilities of the upper-teen years. We'll try to help you use their questions and experiences together with reliable physiological information, as you work through what it means to be a sexual, Christian human being.

The Bible gives us the basis and the standards for our life with God, our relationship with others, and our attitudes about our own sexuality.

So it is, that through the upper-teen years and all through life, the encouraging thing is that God really is "Lord of Life and Lord of Me."

Chapter 1
Sex and Sexuality

SEX IS ... SEXUALITY IS

In your opinion, which of the following is the best definition of sex? The second-best? The third-best?

* a physical desire
* being male or female
* a gift of God
* a subject nice people don't talk about
* sexual intercourse

The word "sex," strictly speaking, is the quality of being male or female, depending on the physical makeup of the individual.

Comparisons are often tricky, but one way to define sex might be to compare it to a new car.

A new car has wheels, bolts, gears—all the parts that are necessary for a car to run.

A person has male or female hormones, male or female sexual organs—all the parts that are necessary to function as a man or a woman.

A new car is good. When you have one, you're proud of it.

Your sex is good. It is a gift from God, something to be proud of.

In order to say and appreciate what your sex adds to your whole life and character, you usually use the word: sexuality. Let's take the comparison a step further:

A new car doesn't mean much if it just sits in the driveway. It's how you use it and take care of it that counts.

Your sexuality includes your sex organs—as well as the way you think and feel about them and use them. It takes into account everything you are as male and female.

Like anything else, cars and sex can be used responsibly— or they can be abused . . . or they can be misused. If we drive our cars or use our sex to hurt others, God may forgive us, but His forgiveness does not take away the consequences of our actions. The run-over pedestrian is still dead; the unmarried pregnant girl is still pregnant.

Driving recklessly may look like fun, but it isn't in the long run. Damages and injuries are hardly fun.

Sexual irresponsibility may look like fun, but it isn't in the long run. Guilt and broken relationships for ourselves and others are hardly fun.

Eight-year-old Jason might think he's driving when Dad lets him make believe he's steering the car. But driving is a lot harder— and a lot more interesting— than steering.

People who just think of sex (body only) instead of sexuality (all of you—body and spirit) miss the greatest gift: a deeply satisfying relationship with another human being.

12

SEXUALITY IN THE MEDIA

What attitudes about sex do you see reflected in
* the magazines you read (or look at)?
* the movie you saw most recently?
* your favorite TV show?
* the songs in the current top ten?

Do these show responsible, sexual persons, who, though imperfect and vulnerable, do have a set of values—or do they picture glamorous figures who live in a world of fantasy? Does the story tell of trust, communication, and caring between two loving people—or does it imply that physical attraction is all there is?

Many ads, movies, TV shows, etc. are aimed at the "lowest common denominator." They seem to be written for the lowest level of maturity and intelligence.

If we constantly fill our minds with words and pictures that show sex as an aggressive and impersonal act, we may find it hard to maintain our own moral values and to develop lasting, loving relationships.

On the other hand, we can learn from movies, books, and other media that honestly describe a growing relationship between two real people, even if those people act in ways we might disagree with. We can learn from both the good and the bad choices of others.

Even when a book or a movie reflects real life with reasonable honesty, you may not agree with the writer as he/she speaks through the characters. For example, in a story from a popular 1970s TV series, Phyllis meets an old girlfriend of her late husband Lars. Even though the relationship was over long before her marriage, Phyllis is jealous. She wonders how intimate Lars was with this attractive woman and finally asks her point-blank: "Did you ever go to bed with Lars?"

The meaning of the answer is clear. "I dated Lars several times a week for eight months. What do *you* think?"

* What does the implied statement "of course sexual intimacy goes with dating" tell you about the writer's values?
* Have you seen any other movies or TV shows that give the same "everybody does it" message?
* What effect might this subtle message have on a person who has not thought through his or her own values?

MASCULINITY AND FEMININITY

Which of the following phrases describe a "real man"? Which describe a "real woman"? Which could describe both?

is a good cook
is competitive
is sensitive to others' feelings
is aggressive
is athletic
is independent
is courageous
is a leader, a "take-charge" person
cries easily
cries when very sad
can change a tire, use power tools, do minor repairs
can clean, sew, do laundry
can speak and write well
likes touching, tenderness
likes pretty, colorful things

TRADITION VS. CHANGE

The way you answer the above will depend mostly on what you have become accustomed to. Traditionally, people have had very definite ideas on roles for men and women. In our culture, men were expected to be the leaders at home and in society. They were expected to be wise, strong, and brave at all times— never showing emotion, never needing help. It was assumed that women's lives were centered on their homes; they were protected, guided, and supported by their men.

The big advantage of the traditonal system was that everyone knew exactly what was expected of him or her. Life may have been dull sometimes, but at least you knew what was expected of you.

In today's world, changes have taken place. You can decide how you will act as a male or a female. For instance, Amy loves to cook. She looks forward to making a home for her husband and children some day. But Peg loves to work with electronics. Whenever she daydreams about the future, she imagines a career as an engineer.

On the other hand, Bob enjoys being with Gail, who shares his interests—art, music, and serious conversation. The first time Gail beat Bob in tennis, it bothered him; then he realized he doesn't have to be tops at any sport to prove he is a man. He used to pretend to be tough and unemotional. Now Gail encourages him to show his real feelings. She admires him for his honesty.

Although these young people are very different from one another, all of them are normal. As long as they recognize that they do have choices, they will not be trapped by inflexible ideas of what male or female should be. They can be free to be honest with themselves, to stay in touch with their own feelings about manhood or womanhood. Each person can choose his or her own version of what it means to be a man or a woman.

BEGINNINGS OF SEXUALITY

You began to be a "real man" or a "real woman" at the moment of conception, about nine months before you were born. At your birth your parents joyfully said, "It's a boy!" or "It's a girl!" Their announcement was based entirely on the way your body was made. Almost all other differences between boys and girls come later. They are learned.

From the day of your birth, everyone treated you as a boy or a girl. By the age of two you were watching others of your sex very carefully so you could imitate their walk, mannerisms, or speech. Your *gender* (being male or female) is so firmly a part of you that nothing can shake your deep knowledge of who you are.

Nothing, that is, but other people. If you believe the myths that say "women always . . . " or "a man would never . . . ," you may face serious problems someday. Real men just can't live up to the "macho man" fantasy all the time. The man who tries will pay with ulcers and/or damaged relationships with those close to him. The woman who tries to match a fantasy picture of "perfect wife and mother" often becomes frustrated and stops growing as a person.

CHOOSE YOUR OWN ROLES

It's not easy to sort out today's conflicting definitions of masculinity and femininity.

Men hear these conflicting statements today:

"Only cowards back off from a fight."

"Peace on earth is sometimes more important than winning."

"Never show weakness. Above all, *never* cry."

"A healthy male is someone who freely expresses his feelings and emotions."

"It's unmanly to cook, clean, or take care of children. That's women's work."

"The husband who can't cook and do laundry needs a mother, not a wife."

Women hear these conflicting statements today:

"You must have a career to fulfill yourself."

"It is your duty to stay home and care for your children."

"Be assertive and competitive. Men will take advantage of you if you let them."

"Although we are equal to men, we are different. Each sex has its strengths and weaknesses."

"The man in your life, your father or your husband, will take care of you."

"Every woman must prepare for the day when illness, death, or divorce may suddenly force her to become independent."

As you sort through statements like these, take a hard look at the ones that pretend that all men or all women are alike. If you study the people around you, you will probably discover that there are at least as many differences between any two men or any two women as there are between men and women as groups.

Your masculinity or your femininity is an unshakable part of every cell in your body. When you are sure of something, you no longer have to prove it. You are free to be yourself.

Chapter 2

The Male and the Female Sexual Systems

Girls ask:

Why am I developing slower than my girlfriends?
How can a penis fit in a vagina?
Am I supposed to be menstruating at the same time every month?

Guys ask:

Is it normal to have wet dreams?
How come I get an erection when I'm not thinking about sex?
Why aren't penises all the same size?

Many young people "know" more about sex than adults, but often their information has some half-truths and myths mixed in. This chapter will give a quick review of the facts you already know, with special attention to common questions asked by teens.

THE MALE SEXUAL SYSTEM

All things were created by Him, and all things exist through Him and for Him. Romans 11:36 TEV

The Testicles

The *testicles* are roundish glands that hang just behind the penis in a pouch called the *scrotum*. Why is the left testicle lower (and sometimes larger) than the right one? Is this a mistake in God's creation? No—it's really a miracle of design, for it keeps the testicles from getting hurt as your legs come together.

Consider, too, God's wisdom in putting the testicles in the scrotum—*outside* the rest of the body. In this way the testicles

17

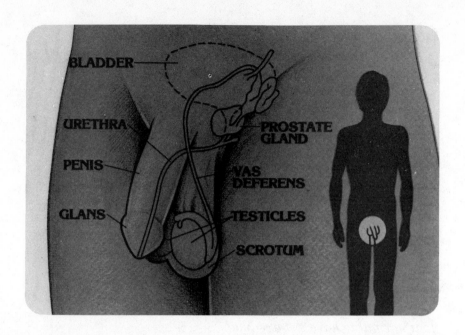

are able to maintain the temperature they need—about 4° lower than the rest of the body. In cold weather the muscles of the scrotum contract to bring the testicles close to the body. In warm weather the muscles relax to lower the testicles away from the body. In this way the testicles are always kept near the proper temperature.

A boy's testicles are inside his body until a few weeks before he is born. Then the testicles descend into the scrotum. In about 3% of boy baby births, one or both testicles do not come out into the scrotum. Although a doctor's help is needed to correct this condition, these boys are usually normal in every other way.

The testicles produce *sperm*, tiny cells that are needed for reproduction. From puberty into old age, these amazing glands make millions of sperm a day. Sperm can be seen only through a microscope; one drop of fluid can contain 120 million of them. They look like tadpoles with skinny, active tails.

Another important job of the testicles is to produce *testosterone*, a *hormone* or chemical that controls the development of male sex characteristics—like a beard and lower voice. During puberty, boys notice that the testicles and penis grow and become darker in color; hair grows in the pubic area and later on the body and face; the voice deepens; and muscles and bones grow very rapidly. Suddenly boys are interested in girls in a new and exciting way.

18

The Sperm Storage and Transportation System

After sperm are produced in tiny tubes inside the testicles, they move to larger tubes, where they mature. Then they travel through another tube (the *vas deferens*) to the *seminal vesicles*, which are two pouches just behind the bladder. Next to the seminal vesicles is an active little gland, the *prostate*. It constantly manufactures a fluid that mixes with fluids from other glands to make *semen*.

VAS
DEFERENS

Semen is the white, sticky fluid in which sperm leave the penis.

Only 1-3 teaspoons of semen leave the body at any one time. There is no truth to the story that a discharge of semen in any way weakens a man.

The Penis

The penis hangs in front of the testicles. Like the testicles, the penis is very sensitive to contact. The *glans*, the end of the penis, is especially sensitive. It is covered with a loose elastic skin, the *foreskin*.

Many doctors recommend *circumcision* (removing the foreskin) to prevent dirt or urine from collecting under the

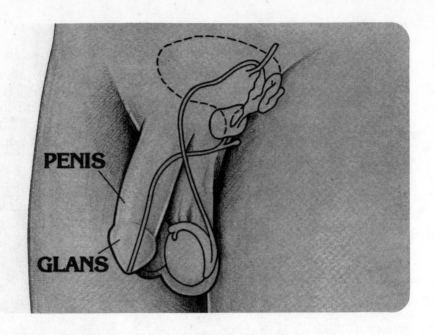

foreskin and thus causing infection. Usually this simple operation is done soon after birth, but it can be done at any age.

Beginning with Abraham, males among God's Old Testament people were circumcised by God's command as a reminder of the special relationship they had with God. Joseph and Mary took Jesus to be circumcised when He was eight days old. Today the church observes the circumcision and naming of Jesus on January 1 each year.

Circumcision does not affect a male's ability to give or receive sexual pleasure.

Erections

When a man is sexually aroused, the soft, limp tissue of his penis becomes *erect* and larger—hard enough to stand away from the body. Even though there is a difference in the size and shape of penises, there is little difference in the sexual satisfaction for either man or woman.

The inside of a penis is a lot like a sponge. During an erection extra blood rushes into the penis. Valves close to hold this blood under pressure.

Erections can happen at any age, but they seem to happen more often during adolescence. They can be caused by sexual feelings and daydreams, but they also occur because of tight clothing, pressure from a full bladder—or even for no apparent reason. Although it can be very embarrassing when it happens in public, it is usually not very noticeable to other people.

Ejaculation

If the stimulation that causes an erection is continued, semen moves into the *urethra* tube. Strong muscles move it along until it squirts or oozes from the penis. This *ejaculation*, or squirting out of semen, goes along with intense feelings of pleasure, called an *orgasm*. Although semen and urine both leave the body through the urethra, they cannot pass through the penis at the same time. Special muscles close off the bladder when the penis is erect.

When the seminal vesicles are full, ejaculation may take place during sleep. This is called a *nocturnal emission*, or a "wet dream" because of the sex dream that may happen during the ejaculation.

Sometimes young men feel guilt or embarrassment about nocturnal emissions. Yet they are completely natural. They are part of God's design for relieving sexual tensions and releasing surplus semen.

THE FEMALE SEXUAL SYSTEM

All things were created by Him, and all things exist through Him and for Him. Romans 11:36 TEV

The Internal Sexual Organs

Deep inside the female body is a pair of *ovaries*. They contain thousands of undeveloped egg cells. When a girl is 10 or 12, her ovaries begin to produce *estrogen*, the female hormone that controls many changes in her body.

During the next few years her breasts develop and her hips broaden. Her height and weight increase fast. And her sex organs grow. Hair appears under her arms and in her pubic area. As menstruation begins, she may also notice a clear whitish discharge from her vagina.

At puberty the egg cells in the ovaries begin to ripen. About once every 28 days, a ripe egg cell leaves one ovary and moves into the *fallopian tube* next to it. Egg cells cannot move by themselves. They are carried along by fluids or by tiny hairlike *cilia* on the inside of the tube.

Fertilization, the uniting of a mature egg cell with a sperm cell, almost always happens in the fallopian tube. Immediately the covering of the egg cell changes to block the entry of other sperm. The new cell that has been created moves slowly into the *uterus*.

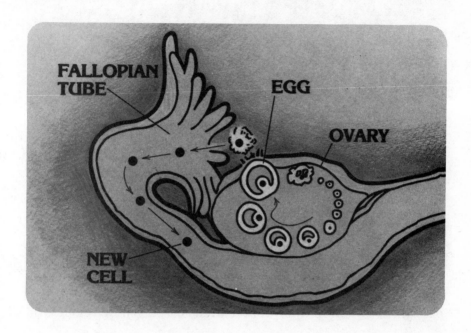

In a mature woman, the uterus is about the size and shape of a large pear. The walls of the uterus are made of extremely elastic muscles, able to stretch to an enormous size during pregnancy. These same powerful muscles contract downwards to make childbirth possible. They also contract during menstruation, sometimes causing cramps in some women.

The *vagina*, or birth passageway, is a tube also made of elastic muscle. The walls of the vagina touch each other most of the time, much like a collapsed balloon. During sexual excitement the vagina expands and produces a lubricating fluid that makes intercourse easier.

The *cervix*, or neck of the uterus, which opens into the vagina, is made of muscles that close tightly during pregnancy, but stretch enormously during childbirth. No human engineer could design such a perfect system for beginning and supporting a new life! It's another miracle by God, the master Designer!

VAGINA

The Vulva, or External Sexual Organs

The opening of the vagina is partly covered by the hymen, a membrane that is broken the first time sexual intercourse occurs. At one time an unbroken hymen was an important proof of virginity. We now know that it often is broken much earlier in

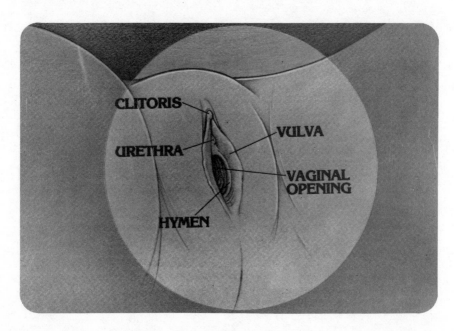

CLITORIS

URETHRA

HYMEN

VULVA

VAGINAL OPENING

life without the girl realizing it. Because some hymens are thicker than others, many women choose to have theirs checked by a doctor and stretched or cut if necessary before they are married.

Surrounding the opening to the vagina are two fatty folds of skin, the *labia majora* (major lips). The outer sides are covered with hair. They serve as protection for the genital area.

Inside these are two more folds of skin, the *labia minora* (minor lips). Sometimes they are hidden by the major lips; sometimes they stick out between them. They may be pink or brown, wrinkled or smooth.

At the top of the labia minora is a small cylinder of very sensitive tissue, the *clitoris*. A woman may be able to see the pea-sized end of it with a mirror, or it may be hidden by the folds of the labia.

Between the clitoris and the vagina is the *urethra*, where urine leaves the body. It is very small and is completely separate from the vagina.

MENSTRUATION

Which of the following common myths have you heard?

1. Menstruation is dirty because bad blood is leaving the body.

2. Menstruation is an illness. A menstruating woman should avoid exercise, especially swimming.

3. The menstrual cramps some women complain about are imaginary.

4. Women cannot handle important jobs because their menstrual cycle produces mood changes and uneven levels of energy.

5. It's difficult for teenage girls to use tampons.

The above statements are *all false*. Don't be embarrassed if you have fallen for one or more of them. They are so widely believed that nearly everyone is affected by the attitudes they represent. Because there is a kernel of truth in each of them, you need detailed, factual information to separate the truth from the myth.

Here it is:

Facts About Myth 1: The menstrual flow is a mixture of blood and cell fragments. When a ripe cell leaves the ovary, the uterus prepares for the possible beginning of a new life.

25

Hormones (estrogen and progesterone) cause a soft thick lining to form on the uterus walls. Extra blood flows to the uterus, ready to nourish a fertilized egg.

When fertilization does not happen, the egg cell, the new lining, and the extra blood are not needed. They break up and flow out through the vagina. This process happens about once a month for 25-40 years. Since God doesn't turn out "production line" people who are exactly alike, the menstrual cycle is a little different for each woman.

Although menstruation is a normal, healthy process, some girls are embarrassed by it, especially in the early years. This feeling usually changes when they become more used to their adult bodies.

Perhaps the "dirty" label began because of the odor that forms when air and warmth *interact* with the menstrual flow. If a woman keeps herself clean and changes sanitary napkins or tampons frequently, odor will not be a problem.

Facts About Myth 2: Menstruation is a sign of a healthy, normal body. Although many women have times when they feel uncomfortable during their periods, they can and should carry on normal activities. Many Olympic athletes have given top performances while menstruating.

A woman should avoid being chilled during menstruation, and should probably exercise moderately rather than strenuously. She'll feel better if she follows ordinary health rules, like getting enough rest, drinking plenty of fluids, and avoiding rich foods.

Facts About Myth 3: Menstrual pain is real but not universal. For 30%–50% of women, hormonal changes just before menstruation produce a variety of symptoms called premenstrual syndrome (PMS). The most common are a dull abdominal ache, a feeling of fullness, and breast tenderness. Women who notice PMS symptons should cut down on salt, sugar, and caffeine during the week before menstruation.

Studies show that daily exercise will, after several months, give definite relief to about two thirds of the women who suffer from menstrual pain. The removal of tension also helps. Saying to yourself, "Relax, dummy!" may not be the answer. However, it is important to understand that your mind and your body do work together. If you expect to feel pain, you are more likely to react fearfully to that first little cramp, with more tension bringing more cramps. So encourage yourself; remind yourself that you are experiencing a God-created readiness to bring new life into the world.

If you are one of the 5% of menstruating women who experience severe PMS symptoms, see a doctor. Doctors can prescribe drugs that may not only give relief from pain but help correct the hormone imbalance that may be the cause of the symptoms.

Facts About Myth 4: Other symptoms of PMS may include tension, depression, or fatigue. Many women feel extra energetic or exceptionally happy midway between two menstrual periods, when a mature egg leaves the ovary. The extra hormones produced at that time can boost her energy level and make her feel good all over. Two weeks later her hormone level drops—just before she begins to menstruate. She may feel tired and somewhat depressed. However, there are other body cycles that have a similar effect— and these apply to men as well as women. We all need to learn about ourselves and to adjust to these changes and make the most of every day.

Facts About Myth 5: In most girls the hymen stretches easily enough to permit use of a tampon. However, a girl must know her own body well enough to place the tampon correctly.

Carefully study the diagrams on page 24. Notice that the vagina is halfway between the clitoris and the anus, and is directly behind the urethra. Move the tampon a bit to find the opening in the hymen. Push the tampon all the way in, past the muscles at the opening. It cannot go too far or fall out. Relax and take your time. Nervousness may cause the muscles around the vaginal opening to tighten.

Many women prefer sanitary napkins or pads. They also work very well except in special situations like swimming. There are two types, one worn with an elastic belt, the other with adhesive backing that sticks to underpants.

Your physician will be happy to answer any questions regarding the use of tampons or other sanitary protection.

MORE QUESTIONS

What if a vagina is too small for a penis? (Judy, 16)

The walls of the vagina are elastic enough to permit the birth of a baby; an erect penis is much smaller. When a woman is sexually aroused, her vagina gets bigger and produces a fluid which lubricates the inner walls.

The other boys make fun of me because I have so much fat on my chest it looks like I have breasts. What is wrong with me? (Sam, 14)

There is probably nothing wrong with you. Breast enlargement is very common among adolescent boys. It is a temporary condition and has no connection with your masculinity.

Why do people masturbate? (Lisa, 16)

Touching the clitoris, vulva, or penis can produce strong feelings of pleasure. When an individual does it to produce those feelings of pleasure, it is called self-stimulation or masturbation.

There have been many stories told about the harmful effects of masturbation, such as that people who masturbate become mentally ill, get warts, or grow hair in the palms of their hands. These stories are not true. There is no evidence that masturbation causes any *physical* harm.

Persistent masturbation, however, can be the sign that a person needs counseling and help in relating to persons of the other sex as well as assistance in overcoming constant masturbation.

A young person may worry: What do I say and do on a date? What if he (she) thinks I'm weird? What if she (he) doesn't like me? Masturbation can be one way to escape from these feelings of loneliness and uncertainty. It can prevent a person from dealing with these "growing up" problems and solving them with the help that God provides.

In addition, the lustful sexual fantasies that usually go with the masturbation may prevent a person from growing in appreciation of the proper use of God's great gift of sex.

Will masturbation cause problems later in intercourse? (Brett, 17)

Studies show that masturbation ordinarily will not cause problems later in intercourse. One exception: When people learn to reach orgasm very quickly through masturbation, they may have difficulty with premature orgasm in normal sexual intercourse.

My menstrual periods have stopped. I know I'm not pregnant because I'm a virgin. What's wrong? (Julie, 16)

If you have just started menstruating, your body is probably still working on the timing of the menstrual cycle. Many young girls have very irregular cycles. Your periods could be 28 days apart, then 36, then 91, then 27. They will become more regular as you grow older.

Menstrual periods sometimes stop for a while because of unusual stress (a new job, the death of someone close, a breakup with a boyfriend, the loss or gain of a lot of weight). If none of these explanations fit, see a doctor.

I am as flat as an ironing board, and none of the boys give me a second look. Is there something I can do to make my breasts grow? (Sarah, 16)

I'm shorter than the other guys, and my sex organs haven't developed much. Is there something wrong with me? (Tony, 14)

Sarah and Tony are both "late bloomers," people who develop a year or two later than the average. Sexual changes are triggered by each person's individual time clock. Because of this, some 14-year-olds look like adults while others, equally normal, look like children.

Even after they have completed their growing, Sarah's breasts may be smaller than many of her friends' and Tony may be shorter than many other males. Who is to say what is the "right" breast size or height? All of us are different. Many of us are dissatisfied, too, with some of our physical characteristics until we realize that we are lovable and loving people just as we are. God has made us different physically just as He has given us different abilities.

29

Why do so many people think the sexual parts of our bodies are dirty? (Debbie, 15)

Ignorance, mostly. Or maybe they haven't stopped to think about how precisely, how wonderfully, each of us is made. No wonder God thought our bodies good enough to be temples of His Spirit! He made them that way. Adam and Eve were able to be completely naked and unashamed before the fall into sin. Since the fall we have felt differently about our bodies and have had more difficulty seeing them as the gifts of God they really are.

Chapter 3
Sex and Your Health

"I need to have intercourse soon to get experience. What if I get married and can't do it right?"
"I'm too fat to be lovable."
"A few beers make some people irresistible lovers. I hear that marijuana is better yet."
"There are certain drugs that really turn a person on. And there's one—saltpeter—that will take away all sexual desire."
"It's no one else's business if I choose to smoke; after all, it's MY body."
"Nice people don't get VD."

You probably don't believe any of these myths. But they are so common—and so dangerous—that we all need up-to-date information about each of them.

INEXPERIENCE

Myth 1: *"I need to have intercourse soon to get experience. What if I get married and can't do it right?"*
Some young people may worry unnecessarily about not being able to "do it right" when the time comes. But most of the time that kind of "argument" is really an excuse.
People do need to learn how to have intercourse—but two inexperienced married people can learn together. They do need practice—considerate, mutually satisfying practice, which is difficult to have outside the security of marriage, and which God forbids outside of marriage.

OVERWEIGHT

Myth 2: *"I'm too fat to be lovable."*
To be lovable, a person really needs to be loving. God daily

31

gives you the power to be a loving person when He pours out His limitless, unconditional love for you. In Jesus, His Son, He forgives you and calls you His own child.

However, people who are heavier than average often feel so miserably self-conscious that it is very hard for them to take the risk of reaching out to other people.

Mark has been overweight for as long as he can remember. He always walks to classes by himself. He is so afraid of being rejected he won't even join someone who is also alone.

By the time Mark gets home from school, his loneliness and boredom push him straight to the kitchen. He carries a plate heaped with food to the family room, where he watches TV until supper.

Many people are like Mark. To them, food brings relief from feelings like anger, depression, nervousness, or boredom. They know, deep down inside, that they are just making their problem worse, but they can't seem to stop themselves.

Cindy is 17 and has never had a date. She despises herself for her inability to stick to a diet. Like a yo-yo, she loses weight on one new diet after another, but she always puts it back on again. When her older sister teases her, Cindy storms into the kitchen and starts eating chocolate cake. Forty minutes later she is shocked to find that she has polished off the whole thing!

Cindy and Mark's basic problem is not fat, but how they feel about themselves. They need to remember that if God truly loves them, they have reason to respect themselves. In the power of God's love for him, Mark can handle feelings of depression and the after-school blues by

jogging;
taking tennis lessons;
going for a long walk;
writing a detailed description of his feelings (it's one way to talk to God);
calling a friend.

Easy? Not at first. Exercise will certainly help Mark's weight problem and relieve his tension, but it's *hard* for an overweight person. Mark's best bet is to start slowly, working out for short periods every day for the first month or so.

Writing down feelings does help a person understand himself better, but it's a lot of work. Calling a friend is risky; the friend may not feel like talking to Mark today. Is it worth it? His other choice is to continue to let food rule his life.

Cindy can ask God to give her more helpful ways to deal with anger. Any of the options on Mark's list are good choices for Cindy. Or she may decide to confront the person with whom she is angry; she can tell her sister, "I feel both hurt and *furious* when you make fun of me in front of my friends. Please don't do it again!"

As Mark and Cindy realize that "before the world was made, God had already chosen us to be His through our union with Christ" (Ephesians 1:4 TEV), they will begin to like themselves again— and be freed up to *do* something about their overweight.

Support from a group or from one other person can mean a lot to someone who is trying to turn his or her life around. Your doctor can help you plan a diet that will take pounds off and keep them off. A friend can agree to be available for needed encouragement when you are tempted to eat something you shouldn't. Best bet: someone who is dieting too. Even better: someone who has succeeded in losing weight and keeping it off.

Diet groups often include teens. Look up Weight Watchers, Diet Workshop, a hospital eating disorder clinic, or Overeaters Anonymous in your phone book and ask whether a teen would feel comfortable in the group nearest you. Ask about cost too. Overeaters Anonymous is free.

Because your parents care about you, they may be tempted to nag you to join a diet group. Remind them that these groups do no good at all if the person does not want to be there.

Overeaters Anonymous is especially for people like Mark and Cindy, people who can't seem to stop overeating. The OA principles are based on the 12 steps made famous by Alcoholics Anonymous. "We admitted . . . that our lives had become unmanageable . . . We made a decision to turn our will and our lives over to the care of God . . . We made a searching and fearless moral inventory of ourselves." (We note what we eat, how much, and what our real reasons are.) "We sought through prayer and meditation to improve our conscious contact with God . . . praying only for knowledge of His will for us and the power to carry it out."

One more point. If you ask God to help you change your eating habits, you may feel even more guilty if you fall off your diet— "My faith isn't strong enough." God knows how hard it is for you; He forgives all kinds of failures in our lives. His love for you has nothing to do with how much you weigh. If you decide that dieting is not for you, your decision has no effect on your relationship with Him. Fat or thin, you will always be a worthwhile person in His sight.

ALCOHOL AND DRUGS

Myth 3: *"A few beers make me an irresistible lover. I hear that marijuana is better yet."*

Alcohol

Establishing a happy physical and emotional relationship with another person is not easy. It's not surprising that people are anxious to believe that drugs like alcohol will help make it easier. But medical evidence shows that alcohol is not a stimulant; it is a depressant. Why does a drinker imagine he is being pepped up when he is really being slowed down?

Alcohol works first on the brain area that controls judgment and thought. The drinker is more relaxed, thinks fuzzily, has difficulty making decisions.

If a person wants to trap someone—or be trapped—into making a choice he or she would not make while thinking clearly, alcohol is a useful crutch. However, most of us would rather not begin a new relationship of any kind under those circumstances.

Drinking too much can make a man temporarily impotent. The problem usually disappears when he sobers up. However, if impotence is related to a longtime habit of heavy drinking, the problem may be a permanent one.

God's Word reminds Christians that we don't *need* to get drunk. We have a better alternative: "Do not get drunk with wine, which will only ruin you; instead, be filled with the Spirit" (Ephesians 5:18 TEV).

Marijuana

Many people incorrectly believe that marijuana is a sexual stimulant. What it really does is distort a person's picture of reality. Anything that a user believes is true becomes temporarily "real" for him or her.

Evidence from one study suggests that male marijuana smokers may be more likely to be impotent than nonusers. Another study found a definite link between heavy marijuana smoking and reduced levels of sperm and of the male hormone testosterone.

Ephesians 5:18 is a good text to remember also when you're faced with the temptation to use marijuana or any other harmful drug.

34

Reasons Why People Abuse Alcohol and Drugs

The people who are most likely to have an alcohol or drug problem are those who feel they need to drink (or use another drug) to help them through difficult situations.

"I feel so self-conscious at parties. When I'm drinking, I can talk to anybody."

"I smoke pot to escape from the pressures of my life, the problems I have at home and at school."

"When I drink, I don't care about my worries."

We all have pain in our lives. We all have times when we feel lonely or stupid or afraid. Learning to cope with those painful feelings takes time and effort and a continual turning to Jesus. Chemical crutches do not help in the long run.

Next time you feel down, remember that you are not alone. Others are struggling with the same feelings, even though they wear carefree masks. Jesus was an adolescent once. He had the same temptations, fears, and growing pains you face. He understands how you feel. You can talk to Him about it and ask Him to help you. As you depend on His help, you can handle anything.

APHRODISIACS AND ANAPHRODISIACS

Myth 4: *"There are certain drugs that really turn a person on. And there's one—saltpeter—that will take away all sexual desire."*

Androgren is the only effective aphrodisiac (turn on) now known. Although it is a male hormone, it is produced by both men and women. Doctors sometimes prescribe androgen for people whose own bodies do not make enough of it.

Researchers have tested many other drugs for their effect on sexual interest and behavior, but have found nothing conclusive. Our sexuality is too complex to be easily controlled by any one drug. Drugs have different effects on different people, but in general they seem to either have no effect or serve as an anaphrodisiac (turn off).

Some former servicemen tell stories like, "They used to put saltpeter in the coffee so we wouldn't be so interested in girls. I *never* drank coffee!" If the coffee really did have saltpeter in it, it had no effect on anyone's sexuality. Saltpeter is not an anaphrodisiac as was once thought.

DRUGS AND UNBORN CHILDREN

Myth 5: *"It's no one else's business what I do; after all, it's MY body."*

Your body is a gift from God. If you choose to, you can shut Him out of your life.

But the secret of enjoying your body is to give it back! St. Paul urges us to "give Him your bodies, as a living sacrifice, consecrated to Him and acceptable by Him. Don't let the world around you squeeze you into its own mold, but let God remold your minds from within" (Romans 12:1–2 Phillips).

Another point to consider: The body you have been given has within it the mysterious power of conceiving new life. Decisions you make about your body now have a profound effect on children you may have in the future.

A fetus gets the food and oxygen it needs from its mother's body. If harmful chemicals are present in her body, the fetus receives them, too.

Drugs can have a different effect on the fetus than they do on the mother. Certain widely-used tranquilizers (downers) and amphetamines (uppers) can cause birth defects. Even aspirin can be dangerous, taken in the wrong quantities and/or at the wrong time.

Tobacco smoke contains over 250 chemicals, many of them harmful. The evidence about risk to a smoker's own body has been well publicized. However, many people do not understand the damage cigarette smoke can cause to others. Unborn babies are especially vulnerable.

Many of the smoker's red blood cells carry carbon monoxide instead of oxygen. A pregnant woman who smokes cuts off some of her baby's oxygen supply.

Fathers and others who smoke and pollute the air the mother breathes also have a definite effect on the fetus.

The effects of alcohol on the fetus are not definitely known at this time. However, some maintain that even moderate use of alcohol is dangerous, especially late in the pregnancy.

VENEREAL DISEASES

Myth 6: *"Nice people don't get VD."*

What is VD?

Venereal diseases, or VD, are diseases that are usually passed from one person to another by close sexual contact. A more precise name for them is STD: sexually transmitted diseases. The most serious venereal diseases are AIDS, gonorrhea, syphilis, chlamydia, and genital herpes. Other common forms of STD/VD are trichomoniasis and vaginitis (female) and urethritis (male).

Why is VD dangerous?

* People may have VD without realizing it.
* Infected people are misled when symptoms disappear temporarily. However, the symptoms usually come back, worse than before.
* Some consequences of untreated VD can be blindness, arthritis, mental illness, sterility, and/or death.
* Babies born from an infected mother may have major birth defects.

How does a person get VD?

The bacteria, viruses, or parasites that cause VD live on the warm, damp surfaces of the body. The diseases are most often spread by intercourse or intimate sexual activity in which these surfaces touch each other. Because the AIDS virus also lives in blood, AIDS can be spread through contaminated needles used for "shooting" drugs.

In any case, a person who does not have premarital intercourse is far less likely to get VD than one who does. The only sure way to avoid VD is for both partners in the marriage relationship to remain faithful.

Syphilis can be caught by kissing a person who has contagious sores at that time. Gonorrhea can be caught by touching infected sexual organs, if one's hand has a break in the skin. Trichomoniasis can be passed on by moist towels, bathing suits, or a damp toilet seat. In all these cases the infected person may not ever realize that he/she has VD and can pass it on to others.

How can I tell if someone has VD?

You can't. Only a well-informed doctor can tell. A person with a contagious case of VD may appear to be perfectly healthy. On the other hand, the symptoms described in the VD Specifics pages have many other possible causes. You could do someone a great injustice if you assume that his/her illness was caused by VD.

How common is VD?

Very. In routine physical examinations, over 10% of young male soldiers are found to have chlamydia, or nongonococcal urethritis. Almost two million cases of gonorrhea are diagnosed each year. Although only 15,000 new cases of AIDS were diagnosed in 1986, the U.S. Public Health Service estimates that up to three million AIDS cases could exist by the 1990s.

VD SPECIFICS

AIDS

What are the symptoms? (All people may not notice all symptoms.)
Most people have no early symptoms. The AIDS virus attacks a person's immune system and damages his/her ability to fight disease. Without a functioning immune system, the person becomes vulnerable to many life-threatening illnesses, such as meningitis, pneumonia, and cancer. Symptoms of these "opportunistic" diseases include persistent cough and fever associated with shortness of breath or difficulty in breathing and multiple purplish blotches and bumps on the skin. Symptoms of ARC (AIDS-Related Complex) include loss of appetite, weight loss, fever, night sweats, skin rashes, diarrhea, tiredness, and swollen lymph nodes.

How soon do the first symptoms appear?
2 weeks—9 years after exposure

What happens if the disease is not treated?
There is no known treatment for AIDS. The majority of people who carry the AIDS virus show no disease symptoms and may not come down with the disease for many years, if ever. Scientists now predict that 20%–50% of those infected with the AIDS virus will develop a life-threatening, AIDS-caused illness within five years. (The accuracy of all predictions, of course, will need to be evaluated as time passes.)

What will the doctor do?
Diagnosis: Blood test.
Treatment: No cure now known. Avoid behavior that will infect others. (According to present knowledge, the AIDS virus is not transmitted by ordinary social contact, but only through the exchange of contaminated blood, as in using "dirty" needles in "shooting" drugs, and the exchange of body fluids in sexual intercourse.)

Gonorrhea

What are the symptoms? (All people may not notice all symptoms.)
Pain or itching when urinating
Frequent, urgent need to urinate
White or yellow discharge from penis or vagina
Sore penis or vulva
Sore throat
Most women and some men have no early symptoms. Their only hope is that their sex partners will tell them they may have been infected.

How soon do the first symptoms appear?
2–7 days after exposure
Early symptoms last about 2–3 weeks

What happens if the disease is not treated?
Men: The germs spread through the body. If untreated, they can cause any or all of these problems:
Abscess in prostate gland
Swollen, painful testicles
Sterility
Kidney damage
Women: The infection usually centers in the cervix, spreading to all other sexual organs and may cause painful abscesses that leave scar tissue. The scar tissue often blocks fallopian tubes, making pregnancy impossible or very dangerous.
Both men and women may get acute arthritis.

What will the doctor do?
Diagnosis: Examine sex organs. Take a sample of discharge from penis or cervix (an uncomfortable but painless procedure).

Treatment: Give penicillin or tetracycline by injection or by mouth. One dose is usually enough.

Syphilis

What are the symptoms? (All people may not notice all symptoms.)
Stage 1: A sore (usually painless) on the penis, vulva, around the rectum, in the mouth, or on the lips. The sore is at the spot where the infection entered the body.
Stage 2: A rash (sometimes very faint). May turn into sores in warm, wet areas. Temporary hair loss.

How soon do the first symptoms appear?
Stage 1: 10–90 days or more after exposure. If left alone, the sore will go away within a month.
Stage 2: Two weeks to six months after the sore goes away. Without treatment, these symptoms go away within a few weeks or months.

What happens if the disease is not treated?
The patient's syphilis will remain hidden for months or years. Only a blood test can detect it. After 2–40 years have passed, the following symptoms may occur:
Large, destructive sores
Heart problems
Paralysis
Insanity
Irreparable damage during pregnancy

What will the doctor do?
Diagnosis: Examine serum from the sore under a microscope. Take a blood test.
Treatment: Penicillin or another antibiotic. Regular blood tests necessary for one year.

Chlamydia

What are the symptoms? (All people may not notice all symptoms.)
Sixty to eighty percent of women and 25% of men with chlamydia have no early symptoms. Symptoms, when they appear, are similar to gonorrhea (see above).

How soon do the first symptoms appear?
Usually three weeks after infection.

What happens if the disease is not treated?
Men: inflamed urethra and testicles. Possible inflammation of rectum. If untreated, sterility.
Women: Infected urethra and cervix. May cause infertility, pregnancy in the fallopian tube, or inflammation of the pelvis.

What will the doctor do?
Diagnosis: Examine tissue or cell cultures.
Treatment: Give an antibiotic such as tetracycline or erythromycin by injection or mouth.

Genital Herpes

What are the symptoms? (All people may not notice all symptoms.)
Blisters or small bumps on penis and urethra or cervix, vagina, and vulva
May break and form open, painful sores
Pain when urinating (women)
Often the blisters are so small the person does not realize he/she has the disease and can pass it on to others.

How soon do the first symptoms appear?
Soon after exposure.
May go away and reappear months later, even though there has been no sexual contact in between.

What happens if the disease is not treated?
May cause birth defects or death for a baby whose mother has herpes.
Researchers suggest a connection between genital herpes and cancer of the cervix. No cause-effect relationship has yet been proven.

What will the doctor do?
Diagnosis: Check to be sure it is not syphilis.
Treatment: Salve on infected area will make the patient more comfortable. Researchers are still looking for an effective cure.

Trichomoniasis

What are the symptoms? (All people may not notice all symptoms.)
    Women: Yellowish-green smelly discharge
    Pain in pelvic area
    Soreness or severe itching in vulva
    Men: Most have no symptoms.
    Thin, whitish discharge, especially in the morning.
    Tingling, itching sensation in penis.

How soon do the first symptoms appear?
    4–28 days after exposure

What happens if the disease is not treated?
    The tiny parasites that cause "trich" will probably continue to multiply and cause discomfort and other physical problems.

What will the doctor do?
    Diagnosis: Analysis of discharge.
    Treatment: Medication taken by mouth.

How can a person tell if he/she has VD?

An examination by a doctor is the only way to find out for sure. If you notice any of the symptoms, see a doctor as soon as possible. VD is usually quite easy to stop if it is diagnosed early and correctly. DO NOT TRY TO TREAT YOURSELF WITH ANTIBIOTICS OR OTHER MEDICINES. Each disease requires a different treatment.

There are other possible causes for most of the symptoms. For instance, pain during urination may be caused by a kidney or bladder infection. A discharge from the vagina is probably perfectly normal, especially if the woman has noticed no change in the discharge. If you are in doubt, see a doctor. Knowing for sure that you do *not* have VD is important for your peace of mind.

Where can I go for help?

Here are some possibilities.
* *Your pastor.*
* *Your parents.* Most parents are loving, supportive, and forgiving when their teenagers come to them with major problems.

* *Your local public health clinic.* A public clinic is sometimes crowded and impersonal, but in many you will find caring and competent people. Public health doctors see so many VD cases that they become experts in its treatment. There will probably be no charge.
* *Your family doctor.* Level with the doctor. Without information only you can give, he/she may not suggest VD as the possible cause of your symptoms.
* *A trusted school nurse or school counselor.* They will know where you can go for diagnosis and treatment.

Is it ever too late to go for treatment?

Although treatment is much simpler in the early stages, it is possible at any time. (Exception: Researchers are still seeking an effective cure for genital herpes.) In the later stages of venereal disease, treatment will usually prevent further damage but will not undo damage that has already happened.

Are you immune to VD after you have had it?

No. The same person can get it again and again.

How likely am I to get VD?

If you use your sexuality responsibly and wisely, you have very little chance of becoming infected. It's important, however, to inform yourself about VD because
* you may need to advise and counsel friends or schoolmates who are ignorant or misinformed;
* it is possible—though unlikely—for a person who is not sexually active to get VD;
* untreated VD could destroy not only your life, but the lives of your mate and your baby.

Chapter 4

Loved, I Love

"I wish I weren't so shy (clumsy, ugly, stupid)."

"Why should other people like me? Most of the time I don't even like myself."

"I know my sins are forgiven for Jesus' sake. But I don't always FEEL forgiven. I still feel guilty."

"If only I had a steady, everything would be different."

"I know God loves all people. But I am only one insignificant speck compared to the millions of people in the world. I need someone who will care about ME as a person, someone who thinks I am important."

JESUS DEMONSTRATED GOD'S LOVE

One of Jesus' jobs here on earth was to demonstrate to you that God loves you in a very personal way. A leper—Levi the tax collector—a widow—Simon the Pharisee—a prostitute—Jesus made each of them feel important: each of them felt loved.

How many teachers would bother having class if there was a big snowstorm and only one student was there? And yet if you page through the Gospel of Luke you'll notice that Jesus spent a lot of His time teaching or healing just one person.

When you share feelings or problems with God, remember that you are very special in His sight. Incredible though it seems, you have His undivided attention. You don't have to do anything or be anything to get Him to love you. He just does— and He always will. He "did not even keep back His own Son, but offered Him for us all! He gave us His Son—will He not also freely give us all things?" (Romans 8:32 TEV).

LOVED, I LOVE: PRACTICAL STRATEGIES

Key Words

"Jesus makes me God's own son/daughter."

A Situation

Maria stands alone near a group of girls who are waiting for class to begin.

OLD Destructive Response

"I wish I could be their friend. I wish someone would see me and ask me to join them."

NEW Creative Response

"I am God's own daughter. Why shouldn't they be glad to see me? I don't have to try to take over their conversation to make them notice me. I'll just be their friend."

Key Words

"There is more to me than my defects."

A Situation

Randy hates summer. Because he is so tall and skinny he looks ridiculous in shorts. Of course he gets year-round teasing about his big feet.

OLD Destructive Response

"No point in going swimming with the gang when I look like such a freak."

NEW Creative Response

"There is more to me than big feet and bony knees. I have a good sense of humor, and I'm a loyal friend. I can't change my feet, but maybe I'll try weight lifting to build up my muscles. And today I'm going swimming."

Key Words

"God gives me talents."

A Situation

Jenny has an appointment with the manager of a local gift shop. At least 20 girls have applied there for a summer job. Only one will be hired.

OLD Destructive Response

"She's probably already picked somebody. With all this competition I don't have a chance."

NEW Creative Response

"If I were the manager, I'd want a person who is honest, pleasant, hardworking, and dependable. My success in getting baby-sitting jobs proves I meet the last three requirements. And I must have a reputation for honesty, 'cause I'm often asked to take care of the car wash money for the church youth group. God gave me these talents. I know I'd do *well* in that job!"

Key Words

"I know who I am."

A Situation

Brad would like to go around with the "in" group at school. But he is uneasy about some of the things that happen at their parties.

OLD Destructive Response

"If I don't go along, they'll laugh at me. Everyone else does it, so it can't be that bad."

NEW Creative Response

"I know who I am—a person in whom Christ lives. Sure, I want to be part of the group, but not at the price of letting them make decisions for me."

CONVERSATION WITH STEVE: ANGER, GUILT, AND JEALOUSY

I guess I'm just not Jesus' kind of person. I've got this terrible temper, see, and I just don't seem to be able to control it.

For instance?

Last night I half-killed my brother Charley, just because he borrowed my new shirt without asking. That's the worst fight we've ever had, but it isn't the first.

Do they usually start like that? Charley does some little thing you don't like, and then you blow your stack?

I guess so. But it really isn't my fault. Charley acts so superior sometimes, just because he's the lucky one in the family. Everyone thinks he's wonderful because he's smart and good at sports and has the girls falling all over him. He not only thinks he's God's gift to women, but he has the nerve to flirt with MY girl! And he's always borrowing my clothes without bothering to ask. I TRY not to get mad. But I can just hold it in so long, and then ZOWIE! If Charley were more considerate, it wouldn't happen. So it's HIS fault.

Guilt is a very uncomfortable feeling, Steve. People often try to escape feeling guilty by pushing their share of the blame onto someone else. Could that be happening to you?

I guess so. I really feel rotten when I think how much I hurt Charley. And my parents are disappointed in me, too.

Have you talked with God about it?

No. How can I go back and ask for forgiveness again? I keep doing the same thing over and over. If I want to be forgiven, I should stop losing my temper. It's hopeless.

Remember the story of the Prodigal Son? (Luke 15:11-32) The runaway boy was just as ashamed of himself as you are. The sensible thing for his dad to do would have been to take him back on probation: "You can come home if you shape up." But the father ran to meet him, put a ring on his finger, gave a party! That's the way your Father in heaven feels about you.

Even if it's the 27th time I've come home?

That's right. God's love for you does not depend on good behavior, for "it was while we were still sinners that Christ died for us!" (Romans 5:8 TEV)

I can't believe that God approves of my behavior.

You are right. He loves you always—that's *why* He may not approve of all your behavior. He wants you to grow more loving in what you do. He also cares about your parents and your brother, and doesn't want you to hurt them.

But how can I change? I've tried and tried, but it doesn't do any good!

Daily invite His Spirit to live in you and work through you. If you fail sometimes, keep coming back for more forgiveness. Remember, even St. Paul complained that "I don't do the good I want to do; instead, I do the evil that I do not want to do" (Romans 7:19 TEV). So there is a power inside us, leading us to sin. But we have God's own power too. "This power working in us is the same as the mighty strength which he used when He raised Christ from death . . . " (Ephesians 1:19-20 TEV). Stop trying so hard and yield yourself to the fantastic power God gives you as His forgiven child.

You mean it will be easy to control my temper if I have enough faith?

I didn't say that. But your faith is your basic equipment. Trusting God, you can use the thinking ability He gave you. When you stumble, you can learn from your experience. He'll help you, too, to study the strategies other Christians use to handle feelings like anger, and then experiment to find what works for you.

PRACTICAL STRATEGIES: DEALING WITH ANGER, JEALOUSY, AND GUILT

Key Words

"It's OK for me to tell someone I am angry."

A Situation

Charley borrows Steve's clothes without asking.

Possible Responses

Destructive Choice: Hides anger, even from himself. Often leads to a big blowup later.

"I won't say anything. It's not worth arguing about. I'm really not very angry anyway."

Creative Choice: Tells Charley how he feels before he loses his temper.

"Charley, I intended to wear that shirt myself last night. Next time I want you to ask me first. If I'm not here, please find something of your own to wear."

Key Words

"It's OK for me to admit to myself and to God that I'm angry. Then I can choose what to do about it."

A Situation

Charley flirts with Steve's girl Kristen.

Possible Responses

Strategy 1: Steve tells Charley and/or Kristen how he feels. Might work—but Steve has other options if he doesn't want to do that.

Strategy 2: Steve talks it out with a friend—or goes for a long walk and talks to himself. "What am I really afraid of? That I'll lose Kristen to Charley? Do I *really* think that would happen because of 15 minutes of kidding around? No, not if Kristen and I have as good a relationship as I think we do."

Strategy 3: Steve uses hard physical exercise to release his anger. He throws a basketball against the (windowless!) side of a building, goes for a long hard run, or pulls all the weeds in the garden. Or he pounds his mattress, whaps a towel against the bathtub, goes off by himself and yells or cries—anything to get rid of the anger before it becomes destructive.

Strategy 4: Steve prays. God has heard angry feelings before. (Some of King David's Psalms sizzle with his anger: "Strike them with blindness! Make their backs always weak!... May no one be left alive in their tents" (Psalm 69:23-25 TEV). Once Steve has unloaded his feelings, he can ask God to give him power to act with love and understanding.

Key Words

"I can admit to myself and to God that I—like most people—feel jealous sometimes."

A Situation

Steve realizes much of his anger is caused by his jealousy of his brother. He feels that most people (including their parents) like Charley best.

Possible Responses

Strategy 1: Because jealousy is often caused by self-hate, Steve reminds himself that God gives each person different gifts. He asks God to help him learn to appreciate his own special qualities.

Strategy 2: Jealous people often are so busy putting themselves down they don't accept love or compliments from others. "Next time somebody says something nice about me," Steve tells himself, "I won't act like they're either stupid or insincere. I'll just smile and say 'Thank you.' "

Strategy 3: Steve risks talking to his parents about his feelings—not accusing them of favoritism but just telling them how he feels. ("I may be wrong but . . . ")

Sometimes two teens in the same family are treated differently for reasons that have nothing to do with the youngsters themselves. For instance, if Steve's dad is worried about his job right now, he'll show less patience with Steve's low grades this semester than he did with Charley's school problems last year. Usually the inequalities balance out, but we all tend to remember the time when the other person came out on top—and forget the time when the advantage was in our favor.

Key Words

"I can fail without being a failure."

A Situation

Charley says something nasty about Steve's girl Kristen. Steve sees red and starts swinging. Charley's head hits the corner of a table. Cost: 37 stitches and a ruined, bloodsoaked leather jacket.

Possible Responses

Destructive Choice 1: "He had it coming. I don't feel one bit sorry!" (People often make this choice because they think 2 is the only other possibility.)

Destructive Choice 2: "That settles it! I'm no good and never will be."

Better Choice: "Charley should not have said what he did. But that's his problem."

Christian Response: "I am responsible for my own actions. So I'll do my best to make things right with Charley—buy him a new jacket and do his chores until he's feeling better. It's good to know that God never gives up on me, but always forgives and lets me have another chance."

CONVERSATION WITH TRACY: LOVE AND FREEDOM

I'm glad God loves me. But I need somebody human to love me too.

God knows that. His love is the source for human love. Because He loves you, you can risk reaching out to others. You can love and be loved.

But that's what I want! I wish I had a steady boyfriend.

Is a steady the only possible source for love in your life? What about your family and your other friends?

All my girlfriends have steady boyfriends.

And you feel left out. That's natural enough. But if you go steady just so that *you* will feel accepted and important, you are *using* your steady.

What do you mean?

Well, when you like a person for himself or herself, good things can happen. But when you see a person as a means to an end, a way to get what *you* want, you not only destroy the relationship but whatever you get isn't worth much.

Sometimes I'm afraid to face that, I think. I figure I'd better hang onto a boyfriend—even if he's just using me—because if he breaks up with me I'll really feel alone and worthless.

Most of us do have times when we feel like that. The thing we have to get through our heads is that Christ took all that aloneness, all that worthlessness on Himself. All we have to do is turn away from looking inward and center our lives on Him. Then, He promises, "You will know the truth, and the truth will set you free" (John 8:32 TEV).

Free?

Free in Christ. Free to look at yourself honestly and objectively. Free to accept yourself as you are. Free to love and be loved. Free to change. Free to *grow* as God's son or daughter.

Chapter 5
Dating

Does a person have to date to be considered normal?
How does one get started dating?
Is going steady a good idea?
What is the best way to handle a breakup?
How much petting is okay?
What if we've already gone too far?

Questions, questions. There are sure a lot of them when it comes to dating and deciding how far to go on a date.

HELP FROM THE BIBLE

Do you think the Bible has all the answers?
Why don't you do some reading—check it out for yourself? You will not find a Bible text that answers specific questions like, "How does one get started dating?" But you'll sure find guidelines that will help you make decisions.

I don't like being preached at, though.

Who does? But that doesn't make God's law any less true. "The wages of sin"—also sexual sin—"is death." God's Word is very clear about that. The Bible is pretty specific in labeling sexual sins—and warning Christians about them. For example, "God will judge the immoral and adulterous" (Hebrews 13:4 RSV). Or: "Avoid immorality. Any other sin a man commits does not affect his body; but the man who is guilty of sexual immorality sins against his own body" (1 Corinthians 6:18 TEV).

The great thing, though, is that God doesn't just give us warnings. He stands at our side to *help* us. Notice, for example, how that Corinthians passage goes on: "Don't you know that your body is the temple of the Holy Spirit, who lives in you and who was given to you by God? You do not belong to yourselves but to God; *He bought you for a price.* So use your bodies for God's glory" (1 Corinthians 6:19-20 TEV).

What does that mean, "He bought you for a price"?

St. Peter put it this way: "You know what was paid to set you free. . . . It was not something that can be destroyed, such as silver and gold; it was *the costly sacrifice of Christ"* (1 Peter 1:18-19 TEV). *Jesus loved us enough to die for us!* That's what our Christian faith is all about.

It does help me to remember that Jesus loved me that much! And that He gives me His Holy Spirit.

It puts a new light, too, on the false value that says, "Try not to hurt anyone—but if it feels good, do it!"

Yes, that kind of life-style ignores who I am—as a Christian, I mean.

It sure does. You are more than a body. St. Paul lays it on the line when he says: "Your life must be controlled by love, just as Christ loved us and gave His life for us . . . . Since you are God's people, it is not right that any matters of sexual immorality or indecency or greed should even be mentioned among you. . . . live like people who belong to the light" (Ephesians 5:2-8 TEV).

That's a lot to live up to.

It's a way—the only way—to be really free. We don't *have* to do "what everyone else is doing." We're able to say either yes *or* no—remembering who we are as God's own people—and counting on His forgiveness when we fail.

Great! But could we get to some of those specific questions about dating now?

GETTING A DATE

I've been saying "Hi" all semester to a guy in my English class, but that's as far as it goes. How can I get to know him better?

Saying "Hi" with a big smile is a good start. Some days, try to leave class at the same time he does. Ask him a question about the homework assignment; tell him the rumor you heard about the next test; ask what he thinks of the team's chances this season; joke with him. You might gradually become better friends, until one of you suggests doing something together—maybe as a part of a larger group.

It could be, though, that as you get to know each other you'll find you really don't have much in common. That's why it's smarter not to pin all your hopes on one person. Your best bet is to make friends with many people.

It took me weeks to work up courage enough to ask Tracy for a date. She turned me down. What's wrong with me?

Why does there have to be anything wrong with you? If she acted sorry that she couldn't make it, ask her to something else. If she turns you down again without suggesting a different time, etc., forget her.

Everybody is rejected at one time or another. (That's why it's so great to know that God keeps on loving us in Christ!) If you think of something you said or did that may have cooled her interest in you, learn from that. Don't worry about it—her "no" was most likely caused by her interest in someone else or by some other problem in her life.

Value yourself. Remember that you're God's own person. You will find other girls who do appreciate you.

What can I do to make myself more popular?

Many psychologists have conducted experiments that try to find out the reasons why some people have more friends than others. Besides the basic principles we talked about last chapter, the researchers turned up some other factors.

They discovered that the most popular people are those who like others and are pleased when others like them. Yet they are not terribly worried if someone doesn't. (Interesting, isn't it, how this relates to what God intends for us: that we grow as *loving persons!*)

The more relaxed you are, the better you will do in a social situation. It's fatal to allow yourself to worry and fret about what people will think of you. *Expect* them to like you. Why shouldn't they? Concentrate instead on getting to know *them.*

The researchers also found that people make friends with those they see often in pleasant circumstances. You're not going to meet many people while you are in your room at home.

It's nice to be popular. There are times, though, when the price is too high Sometimes it's necessary to choose between doing the right thing and being liked by the group you are in at the time. Often the choice is easier than it looks. The first person to speak up and say "I don't think this is a good idea" may be surprised by the number of others who have been thinking the same thing.

After 6 weeks of looking at Kathy all during history class, I finally asked her out. It was a disaster—neither of us had a good time. What went wrong?

You probably didn't have very much in common. Next time choose a girl you feel comfortable with, a girl who seems to enjoy your company. If you don't know any girls that well, look for a group of guys and girls who do things together. Some people are active members of *two* church youth groups because the groups have so many activities. (No fair freeloading. Do your share of the planning, telephoning, etc., if you choose this option.)

Is there anything wrong with going out on a blind date?

Depends who arranged the date. A friend whose judgment you trust will have a pretty good chance of picking someone you'd enjoy spending an evening with. But when you don't know anyone in the group very well, you are risking an unhappy, embarrassing evening.

What about a pickup date?

There's a real chance of getting hurt—perhaps badly hurt. No one is wise enough to be an instant judge of character. Pickups are often people who want instant satisfaction. Unwilling to spend time and effort building a relationship, they seek "fun" on a one-night-stand basis.

PLAYING THE FIELD

Paul (whom I like fairly well) asked me to the prom. I'll die if I accept and then Ricky (whom I like VERY MUCH) asks me. What should I do?

How would you feel if you were Paul? Would you want to be kept dangling as a "spare" date in case the first choice isn't available? If you want to take your chance on Ricky, give Paul a fast, kind "no, thank you." You don't have to tell him why unless you want to.

If you decide to say yes, play fair. Stick to your yes no matter what happens. If Ricky asks you, you can suggest doing something with him another time.

Is it all right to tell a boy that you like him a lot? I've only gone out with Jim twice, but he already means more to me than any other boy ever has. My friends tell me to play hard to get, but that seems so dishonest.

Playing any kind of game like "hard to get" *is* dishonest. It's silly to pretend to be standoffish unless you really feel that way.

However, you can choose between several ways of letting Jim know you like him a lot. You can push for a steady relationship he's not ready for. If you do, he may be embarrassed and irritated—and might drop you.

A choice made by many girls is to "prove" their love by encouraging sexual intimacy. That's even more dishonest; it's pretending to have the deeply committed permanent relationship people have in marriage. Pretending won't make it true. Most of all, such sexual intimacy is wrong because it leaves God out of the relationship. (Remember all those specific Bible texts we looked at in the beginning of this chapter.)

The best way to let Jim know how you feel about him is to appreciate him. Tell him the strengths and talents you have seen in him. Notice the thoughtful things he does for you; be kind and considerate of his feelings.

Is there something wrong with me because I don't want to date?

Many young people do little or no dating during their teen years. These nondaters usually have friends of both sexes, and they spend time with their friends.

The group gets together for bowling, picnics—whatever. Sometimes closer friendships form within the group—people find others they can talk to, confide in.

The most interesting groups are very flexible about who's "in." New people are welcome, and no one is pressured to participate in any one activity. Often one person will belong to several informal groups. It's a no-hassle way to become more comfortable with people of the other sex.

A girl I've taken out a couple times asked me to a pool party. I wear a brace on one leg. After I remove the brace, I can swim fairly well, but my leg is thin and funny-looking. Will my handicap make a difference to her?

Depends on the girl. Some girls would admire you for dealing with your handicap. Others might be embarrassed and uncomfortable (their problem, not yours). The safest plan might be to tell her about your leg now, so she has time to get used to the idea. Be matter-of-fact, not apologetic. If you have a positive attitude about yourself, chances are others will also.

My father won't let me take a date to a drive-in movie. Why doesn't he trust me?

Maybe he trusts your integrity and your dependability but is a little uneasy about your judgment. What are drive-in movies like in your area? Does more happen in the cars than on the screen? Don't underestimate the power of the temptation to act just as everyone else does. Your father may be concerned, too, about your reputation and that of your date.

If he's wrong about the drive-in movies near you, try to promote a family night out at one of them. Then your dad can see for himself if it's an OK place for you to take a date.

Why should I have to watch out for my reputation just because I'm female? My mother keeps nagging about clothes and makeup that might give people the "wrong idea" about me. But the guy next door does whatever he wants and nobody criticizes him. It isn't fair!

I can appreciate how you feel, but the Bible doesn't make any distinction between men and women when it calls Christians to be as lights in a dark world. How else will people come to know about Jesus—except from Jesus' people? And how interested will they be in what we have to say if we have a bad reputation? Or as 1 Timothy 2:9-10 puts the question: What's more important—fancy and expensive clothes or a loving Christian personality?

I didn't intend to go steady with Sandy, but everyone assumes we are. We've gone out three weekends in a row. I don't want to hurt her, but I don't like this trapped feeling. How do I get out?

Take the risk of sharing your feelings with Sandy. Be sure to make it clear that you really do enjoy her company.

Maybe Sandy has been feeling trapped too. You might be able to work out an arrangement that permits you to see each other without either person feeling tied down.

It's good to get to know a lot of different young women. Why? You'll find out which qualities are important to you in a woman. When the time comes that you are ready to marry, you will choose more wisely.

GOING STEADY

My parents are furious because I exchanged class rings with my boyfriend. In my high school you either go steady or you don't date at all, but my parents can't seem to understand this. How can I get them to see my side?

Most people go with one steady for a few months, then another and another. If you see your relationship as one which is probably temporary, your parents won't worry quite as much.

Explain to your parents that going steady makes it easier to get together casually with a boy. As you do ordinary things together instead of going to the movies, etc., you get to know each other very well. Managing this relationship can be good practice for marriage some day.

Of course, they're probably afraid you may "practice for marriage" in other ways. They have no way of knowing what you're thinking if you don't talk to them—and listen to them. Let them see you've got your head on straight. Let them see how responsible you are about keeping any agreement you make about things like hours, unsupervised time alone together, alcohol, and the places you go.

Right now my girl and I (both 17 years old) think we want to spend the rest of our lives together. But we realize we'll both change a lot in the next few years. How can we keep from getting too serious too soon?

Each of you should have some activities in which you are independent of the other—different jobs, schools, clubs—anything that will help you learn to know yourselves as separate persons. Talk honestly and openly about what is happening in your relationship. Make individual plans for the future, but remind yourselves that joint plans must be tentative. Consciously turn your bodies over to Christ. Together, ask Him to help you guard against hurting each other with too much physical intimacy too soon.

I can't help being very jealous of my boyfriend. One day a note fell out of his pocket. I grabbed it and read it. It was from another girl—a girl I can't stand! It was just about their history

59

assignment, but I was furious! Shouldn't he stop exchanging notes with other girls when he's MY boyfriend?

How do you define going steady? Does it mean a close, caring relationship or does it mean owning another person? Very few people are willing to have no life at all outside a relationship. Even in a marriage, most people do not read their mate's mail unless invited to do so.

Grab hold of God's love for you in Jesus. He will help you feel less insecure. (See Chapter 4 or talk to an older person you trust.)

I have been offered a summer job as drama coach at a camp about 150 miles from home. My boyfriend has a good job right here in town. If I go away, we might not see each other all summer. I need the money and the experience, but is it worth taking a chance on losing my boyfriend?

By the time fall comes, both of you will be more independent, more interesting persons. You'll have many new experiences and ideas to share. You could end up closer than ever.

Even if you stay at home, you are taking a chance that you will lose your boyfriend. People change, especially when they are young. It hurts when a friendship dies, but clinging to each other will make no difference.

If you truly have a strong relationship, it will not wither away because of a summer's separation.

I've been going with Jim for about four months, but lately he's been talking about maybe getting married someday. Even though I like Jim a lot, I'm not ready to even THINK about being serious. I don't want to lose him and I don't want to hurt him. What can I do?

Be honest with Jim. Ask Jesus to help you speak your mind and heart. The conversation could be painful, but it's not fair to let Jim believe you see the future as he does.

But what will happen if you let things go on as they are? Steady dating at a young age often leads to a teenage marriage, especially when the couple feels committed to each other. Five or 10 years later, one or both partners may bitterly regret closing off their options at such a young age and want *out*. Of course many young marriages do succeed (often after a rough struggle). But statistics show that teenage marriages are three times as likely to fail as are marriages of people in their 20s.

By shrinking from painful honesty now, you could store up a lot more pain for both of you—and for possible children—later.

BREAKING UP

I have been in a daze ever since Andy broke up with me. I can't eat, can't sleep, can't study. All I do is sit around and think about him. Help!

The grief that you are feeling is a powerful emotion. You probably feel that you will never be truly happy again. Talk to Jesus about your feelings. Tell Him how it hurts. You may not feel any lightening of your mood, any real sense that He is there . . . *but He is listening, and He does care, and it will make a difference.*

Remember that Jesus often works through other people—including you. Find a trustworthy friend you can talk to about your feelings. If possible establish a new, casually friendly relationship with Andy. When you find yourself thinking about him, remind yourself firmly that this painful time will pass—and *do something else.* This is a good time to get reacquainted with your family, develop new interests, make new friends.

When you do begin dating again, be cautious for a while. Your pride has been hurt. Don't rush into a new relationship; you may unconsciously be using the new person to prove you are still lovable.

PETTING

How far can I go and still have my boyfriend respect me?

Before anyone will respect you, you must respect yourself. Instead of, "How far can I go?" try asking, "What is honest between us?"; "What is best for us?"; *"What honors us as people who belong to God?"*

How can I tell how far I can go with a girl?

Many boys would agree with you that it is up to the girl to decide. Then the boy can follow the macho creed of "get all I can," while he depends on the girl to protect him from a relationship he's not emotionally ready for.

That's not only wrong, it's old-fashioned and immature. What do you want, a sweetheart or a mother? You don't need the girl's no-no to tell you what is right. You have God's Word for your guide. "Have you realized the almost incredible fact that your bodies are integral parts of Christ Himself? . . . Have you forgotten that your body is the temple of the Holy Spirit, who lives in you, and is God's gift to you, and that you are not the owner of your own body? You have been bought, and at what a price!" (1 Corinthians 6:15-20 Phillips)

If you remember that the next time you are in the back seat of a car, you'll have the strength to stay in control and do what God wants you to do.

My girl leads me on and then gets mad when my hands wander. Is she trying to make a fool of me?

Many girls don't realize how quickly and easily boys become sexually aroused. Tell your girl that she's making it very difficult for you to respect the limits you both know are right.

I love my boyfriend very much, and I know he loves me, but I'm afraid of being swept off my feet. What can we do?

Your mutual love can make all the difference—and your mutual love for Jesus, who loves you both. When you truly care for someone, you are not likely to put your own temporary pleasure ahead of the long-term happiness of both persons. When you believe in Jesus, His will and His love for you enters into the relationship.

Remember that the further you go along the road that leads to intercourse, the more difficult it is to put on the brakes and turn around. However, it is *always possible* to stop. You—and your faith in Jesus—are bigger than your feelings.

My boyfriend says he loves me more than I love him, because he's ready for intercourse and I'm not. I'm afraid I will lose him if I don't do what he wants.

You might try talking with him about your relationship to Jesus—and how important His love and His will is in your life—also your next life. If your boyfriend is a Christian, you may be able to explore together what God's Word says about fornication—intercourse outside of marriage. And about the beauty of sexual intercourse within the marriage relationship. (See Chapter 7.)

If your boyfriend is not a Christian and remains insistent, ask yourself: What kind of love for you, really, does he have—if it requires you to give up your relationship to Christ in order to satisfy his physical desires? Is it lust masquerading as love? If he's threatening to dump you "unless you do what he wants"—is this the kind of love you can build a future on? (Prayerfully consider Genesis 39:6-12 and Acts 5:29.)

Ruthie and I went steady for about two years. We thought we loved each other and sincerely intended to get married someday. After we broke up I felt pretty guilty about the heavy petting we had done. Even though we never had intercourse, we came close to it many times.

I've asked God to forgive me, and I know He has. But somehow I don't FEEL forgiven. Why do my guilty feelings keep coming back? Will I always feel guilty about Ruthie, even after I marry someone else?

It is unlikely that the guilt you feel now will be a problem years later in your marriage if you realize you have faced your sin and have been forgiven; you are free to go on with the business of living.

However, you will probably always regret what happened between you and Ruthie. The love you two felt for each other was an honest, real emotion, a gift of God. But the way you expressed that emotion was both wrong and unwise.

It is foolish to assume that teenage love will last forever. Most people have so many new experiences during their teens that they almost certainly will change—in an unpredictable direction. The teenage relationship may well last—but it may not.

Because you acted on the assumption that your feelings would not change, you hurt Ruthie and yourself. God's forgiveness does not instantly erase all consequences. Only time—and God—can heal the emotional damage that happens when people invest so much of themselves in a relationship that does not work out.

How can I get the willpower to say "this far and no further," and stick to it? I feel so guilty sometimes, even though I have never gone all the way.

You need to talk to God about those guilt feelings. Remember, there is no sin so terrible that you cannot ask for—and receive—His forgiveness. He will never, for any reason, stop loving you.

Whatever you've been doing that you feel guilty about—don't do it! Of course that isn't as easy as it sounds, especially when willpower is something you feel you lack. You probably have the will but not the power.

The good news is, the power doesn't have to come from you.

The power comes from the Christ who died for you and rose again. He lives in you. The closer you are to Him, the more power you will have. So read your Bible, pray, commune with Him in His Supper. As you get ready to go out on a date, ask Him to be with you—and trust in *His* power, not your own.

The power He gives you is not a matter of gritting your teeth and being superserious. When things get too intense on a date, often a little humor will relieve the tension. Or you can explain to your date, quite seriously, that you care too much about him (her) to let anything happen you'd both regret.

Chapter 6
Finding Out if Love Is Real

What is the difference between infatuation and real love?

Marriage is a long way off for me—if I decide to marry at all. Why think about it now?

How can we tell if our love will last?

What about these old sayings? Are they true?

"Opposites attract."

"Love at first sight—that's true love."

"A teenage romance is only puppy love."

"If you can't eat and you can't sleep, it must be love."

WILL IT LAST?

Fifteen-year-old Cindy is deeply in love with Mark, and Mark feels the same way about Cindy. They live for the times when they are together. They have a world of their own. They feel intense excitement and pleasure each time they touch or even see each other.

Is their love only infatuation—"puppy love"? No. It is real and genuine. When they promise to love each other always, they both really mean it.

Will their love last? It might. And then again, it might not. At this point in their lives, there's no way to tell. Between the ages of 15 and 21, most people change interests, attitudes, and some values. They discover new talents within themselves. They observe the way others live their lives, and make some decisions about the shape their own lives will take.

Chances are Cindy and Mark will fall in love quite a few more times before they make a final choice of a mate. Each time they will learn more about how to love, how to have a satisfying relationship with another person. They will reevaluate what is important to them. These are times to consciously ask what the will of God is for them and what part He plays in their relationship. Keeping God central will improve their feelings about each other and their understanding of what it means to be male and female.

If love is based mainly on physical attraction, it may not last long. Without mutual liking and respect to keep it alive, sexual attraction withers away.

If you are wondering whether your love is a temporary one, notice the ways in which the relationship has changed you. If people say you have changed, and not for the better—look out! But if you are kinder, more responsible, more self-confident than you were before, you've got a good thing going, at least for this stage in your life. Remember that "in all things God works for good with those who love Him" (Romans 8:28 TEV). God often uses a good relationship with another person to bring out the best in those He loves.

SHOPPING FOR SOMEONE TO LOVE

If you were going to buy a car, you would give that purchase a lot of thought. You would find out the good and bad points of various models. You would decide which features are really important to you. Comfort? Good gas mileage? A low price? Air-conditioning? Your favorite color? Easy parking in a small space? Built-in stereo? You can't have them all, so you do a lot of thinking about your choices. You don't want to spend several years paying for a car you don't like.

Shopping sounds like a coldblooded term to apply to a

human relationship. However, it's not a bad description of a good way to prepare for marriage—even if you decide not to get married at all.

Many single people lead full and happy lives. You might choose not to marry because other things (perhaps your work) are more important to you. But whether you end up getting married or not, you need to think through what you really want your life to be like.

The purpose of this "shopping" is to learn to know yourself and others as developing adults. "Comparison shopping" will greatly increase your chances for a happy marriage. As you get to know different people, you will discover which character traits are really important to you; the kinds of persons with whom you feel most comfortable and happy. You also pinpoint the qualities you absolutely could not stand in a life partner!

Shopping List for Lovers

Here is a "shopping list" of qualities some people think are important in a mate. Which ones are absolutely essential? Which would you consider desirable extras? Which are you indifferent about?

able to handle disappointments without bitterness
able to see the funny side of things
adventurous
affectionate
ambitious
assertive
athletic
attractive
believes in God
can manage money
cares about other people
considerate
dependable
enthusiastic
even-tempered
forgiving
friendly
generous
gentle
good dancer/tennis player/ whatever my main interest
good listener
good self-concept
good talker
hard worker
independent thinker
intelligent
lives his/her faith
loves parties
neat
not a quitter
open-minded
patient
popular
quiet
rich

67

| sense of humor | sexually desirable |
| sensitive, understanding | well-dressed |

Now look at the list in a different way. The key qualities you
have identified are also likely to be important to the person you
might want to marry. What will you have to offer? Do you live
your faith? Are you someone who is dependable, someone whose
word can be trusted? Are you able to laugh at yourself, able to
see the funny side of life? Do you make an effort to be
considerate, to treat people as you would like to be treated? Do
you try to see things from the other person's point of view?

Don't be discouraged if you do not measure up to the
expectations you yourself have for a marriage partner. Work at
improving your weak spots. Building on the strengths you
already have, you can become a person who has many positive
qualities to bring to a marriage. You can become the person God
intends you to be.

Giving yourself enough time and letting yourself become a
little more mature will be helpful. It's well to remember,
though, that age is no guarantee that people will make wise
choices in love. Songs and literature often tell of mature people
who made foolish choices. How then can a couple tell whether or
not their love will last a lifetime? Here are some love signs you
can watch for, some ways to test the durability of your love.

WHAT DO WE HAVE IN COMMON?

The bad thing about our shopping list is that the same
words mean different things to different people. Most of us
would say we want an intelligent mate. But what we really
mean is that we'd like someone who is about as intelligent as we
are, someone who has had about the same amount of education.
When two people of unequal intelligence try to discuss anything,
both are likely to feel bored and frustrated.

The same thing is true of many other words on the list. To
one person *adventurous* might mean a willingness to try a new
restaurant (provided a friend recommends the place). To
another person, *adventurous* might mean a spur-of-the-moment
decision to move to Montana with no job, no money, and three
children. There's nothing wrong with either of those attitudes,
but those two people surely will have things to work through if
they marry.

Often couples are attracted to each other by their differences. If you are a quiet, shy person you might enjoy going out with a "life of the party" type to help overcome your shyness. Don't count on it working though. What often happens is that the quiet one is dragged to parties by the social one, or the social one sits unhappily at home with the quiet one.

Another common difference is family background. What will happen if Lori and Stu fall in love? Stu's family life is lively, warm, and loud. Stu is the only one who has graduated from high school. There isn't much money, but there's always an extra bed for a cousin from the country or a foster child who needs love.

In Lori's family, books and travel have always been important. Both of her parents have interesting, demanding careers. They are active in church and community affairs. Home is a quiet, restful place for relaxed conversation and listening to music.

Many couples as different as Stu and Lori have built happy marriages—and many more have failed. Couples who are thinking of marriage should spend as much time as possible with each other's families. Differences may grow smaller as they get to know each other better. Or they may find the differences eventually kill the love they shared. What one enjoys as a novelty doesn't always satisfy as a steady diet.

WILL MARRIAGE CHANGE US?

One of the things Julio loves about Maria is her enthusiasm. Whatever Maria does, she goes all out. Right now she's all wrapped up in dancing. Determined to be a professional dancer, she spends all her free time practicing—plus some time her parents want her to spend on homework and family responsibilities.

"She'll settle down after we are married," Julio figures. "Of course she'll want to continue dancing, but she'll also work and clean. Maria's love for me is stronger than her love for dancing."

Julio may be in for a surprise. It's unfair of him to attach unspoken conditions to his love for Maria. Although people can change, it's unrealistic to suppose that getting married will make it happen. Julio and Maria need to talk frankly about what each of them expects from marriage.

It's good that Maria has been open with Julio about the

69

family conflicts caused by her intense desire to dance. Love often makes a person conceal some qualities or interests, lest they cause rejection by the loved one. That is both unwise and dishonest. It's important to set standards of appreciation, consideration, and unselfishness you are willing to live with for the rest of your life.

God's Holy Spirit enables Christians to grow in all the qualities that make a marriage a growing and happy relationship: "love, joy, peace, patience, kindness, goodness, faithfulness, humility, and self-control" (Galatians 5:22-23 TEV).

COMMUNICATION

In the best marriages communication begins long before the couple heads for the church. Many hours need to be spent on the building of a friendship, talking about—
> your faith in Christ and how this relates to—
>> your complete life histories
>> your feelings about yourselves, your families,
>>> your interests, your sexuality,
>>>> your goals.

There's more to communication than sharing life histories and future plans. Communication starts with activities, loving listening to everyday problems and feelings. Here's an example of what we mean:

Nancy was late getting to the football field. Everything had gone wrong during the day. The final straw was when she was stuck at a railroad crossing with a freight train stopped in the middle of it. She was angry and upset with herself. She raced to the stadium gate, where Jack paced up and down looking at his watch.

Jack: Hi, honey! How's it going?
Nancy: OK, I guess.
Jack: Where've you *been*? The game's about to start. Hurry, let's get to our seats.
Nancy: Don't *rush* me!
Jack: It's bad enough being late. You don't have to be nasty about it!
Nancy: Find someone else to sit with. I'm going home!

Nancy probably hadn't even admitted her angry feelings to

herself. Jack had no idea what was going on inside her head—
until it was too late!

What if Nancy had kept in touch with her own feelings?
And if Jack had listened in a loving way? What might have
happened then?

Jack: Hi, honey! How's it going?

Nancy: Terrible. I feel mad at the world.

Jack: You had a bad day?

Nancy: You know that math test I was worried about? I
flunked it.

Jack: You began the day with bad news, huh?

Nancy: And then, in English class, Mrs. Hobson jumped
all over *me* because the girls next to me were
talking. I didn't have time to argue with her
after class because I had to go straight to work.
And then we were so busy I had to work an extra
30 minutes. I *knew* I'd be late for the game! And
then I was stopped by a train.

Jack: No wonder you were upset.

Nancy: I sure was. But I feel better talking about it.
Thanks for listening.

WHAT HAPPENS WHEN WE FIGHT?

People who are in love still do have disagreements just like
anybody else. Some couples are afraid to talk honestly. "If I tell
her about that, she'll be angry." "If I tell him what I've decided
to do, he'll try to stop me." Each tells the other only what he or
she wants to hear. Each is very careful to cover up problems
before they cause any unpleasantness.

When a disagreement does surface, each person may be
surprised and hurt by the other's "unreasonable" anger. And
terrible, wounding things are said by both persons.

Talking through disagreements is a lot easier than letting
them get to the point where something that may be relatively
minor tears you apart. But as Christians you can trust each
other to not intentionally hurt each other. And you can offer
forgiveness to each other when you slip and say or do something
to hurt or offend.

The secret is learning to make conflicts work for you
instead of against you. You will become a little closer each time
you settle a problem in a way both partners can live with.

There are several ways to deal with conflict. For example, one person may give in:

Herb: Let's go to the movies tonight.

Sheila: I really had my heart set on staying home, but if it's important to you to go out tonight, I'll go.

Or it may be possible to work out a compromise that meets both people's needs:

Pete: Let's go to the movies tonight.

Sarah: I really had my heart set on staying home, but if it's important to you to go out tonight, I'll go.

Pete: I'd like to go out, but if you want to stay home, maybe I will come over and watch a movie on television with you.

Sarah: That sounds like a pretty good idea.

Sometimes you will not be able to agree on certain issues. That can be a real test of your love and trust for each other. It's a time to say, "I love you even if I don't agree with you." If you can practice this kind of acceptance with people around you, it will be a lot easier to do in a marriage relationship. You don't always have to agree about everything. (Of course, if the issue involves a matter of right and wrong, a clear command of God, you will want to keep on witnessing for the right, striving lovingly to change the other person's point of view and praying for God's Spirit to work through your witness.)

CAN WE TALK TO EACH OTHER WITH COMPLETE HONESTY?

One of the joys of a good relationship is having someone to talk to. The freer you feel to share about yourself with another person the closer you will feel toward that person. All of us are at different levels, though, when it comes to what we think is complete honesty. You may want to share your innermost thoughts. The other person may have to think through an issue before sharing it with anybody.

WHAT IF WE BELONG TO DIFFERENT CHURCHES?

The question may be: Can a marriage work if the partners are of a different religion? Yes, but it's not easy. The ideal is to be equally committed to Christ and both belong to the same church so that you can share your faith completely. Christ should be the cornerstone of a relationship—certainly of a marriage. It is unfortunate when one or the other cannot share Him because of differences in belief or denomination.

Remember that if you want a Christian marriage, marry a committed Christian. A marriage that is built on a deep trust in and communion with God is like no other relationship on this earth. When both partners seek God's will in their lives, they are not alone in their struggle to make their marriage work. Their shared faith is the basis for all goals, all values, all decisions. God provides them with the strength they need when trouble comes; He guides them to the abundant life He wants for all of us.

Chapter 7

When Two Become One

What actually happens in sexual intercourse?
What difference does marriage make in a sexual relationship?
How often does a married couple have intercourse?
What is the secret of a happy marriage?

WHAT HAPPENS IN SEXUAL INTERCOURSE?

Sexual intercourse is more than placing the penis in the vagina. There is a time before intercourse when the couple stroke, touch, gently massage, and kiss each other's bodies. This is called foreplay. Ideally, they have talked about what arouses each of them and know which areas of the body to stimulate. These areas, called erogenous zones, are a little different for each person. Typically they include the sex organs and the areas around them, the nipples, inner thighs, mouth, lips, neck, earlobes, eyelids—all areas with many nerve endings.

As the couple becomes more and more excited, heartbeat and blood pressure go up dramatically. Muscles tense. In some people, a measles-like flush covers part of their bodies. In about 60% of men and nearly 100% of women, nipples become erect and enlarged.

Blood rushes into the man's penis and stays there, making it erect and hard. The woman's vagina expands and "sweats," producing a lubricating fluid that makes intercourse easier. The muscles at the entrance to the vagina relax. Her clitoris enlarges at first, flattens out, and then seems to disappear under the fold of skin that ordinarily covers most of it.

When both partners are ready, they work together to guide the penis into the vagina.

In our culture, the woman usually lies on her back with legs apart and knees bent. The man faces her, supporting his body on his elbows and knees. As the penis moves back and forth inside the vagina there is friction on the clitoris caused by the movement of the labia.

Their excitement may build until one or both of them experience orgasm. The man's penis ejaculates semen; the woman's vagina contracts and expands several times; they tremble with intense physical and emotional pleasure.

Then all of the signs of arousal go away. A feeling of well-being and complete relaxation floods their bodies. This can be a special time of tenderness when they can lie in each other's arms, caressing and talking.

Is it always like that?

No. Different couples have different preferences about such things as foreplay and position during intercourse. There are many variations.

People have described intercourse as thrilling—soul-stirring—boring—shocking—deeply satisfying—painful—wonderfully comfortable—humiliating—confidence-building—disappointing—fascinating—disgusting—delightful.

How can the same experience be so different for different people?

God intends intercourse to be a superbly joyous way to

express mature committed love between a man and a woman. In many different places the Bible speaks very positively of sexual intercourse—always within marriage. (Different words are used to describe sex outside of marriage.) Does this mean that sex within marriage always feels wonderful, and sex without marriage always feels terrible?

It isn't quite that simple. Researchers are finding that sex without commitment tends to be flat and joyless compared to sex within a good marriage. Notice the word "good." Marriage alone does not do it. More is necessary.

WHAT THINGS MAKE A DIFFERENCE IN SEXUAL PLEASURE?

The couple's total relationship controls their ability to give and receive sexual pleasure. Before intercourse can be the great experience it is meant to be, couples need to have complete trust, complete confidence in each other. They need to know that they are loved. Then each is free to suggest having intercourse, and each can say "some other time," without the other feeling rejected.

If a man and a woman try to use intercourse to become closer to each other, they will be disappointed. It works just the opposite. In intercourse, a couple celebrates the unity, the concern for each other's needs, that already is there.

Even within a good relationship, the quality and intensity of a sexual experience varies greatly from one time to another. Sometimes the pair will come to orgasm together, sometimes separately. Sometimes one person will enjoy intercourse, but will not come to orgasm at all.

For most women and many men, the most important part of a sexual relatonship is emotional intimacy. Their deepest needs are met by tenderness, closeness, and sharing.

Couples sometimes use a "how to" book about sex as a report card rather than a guide. If their experience does not follow the book, they feel like failures. These feelings matter. Fear of failure can interfere with the normal physical reactions of the body. Fear can prevent a man from having an erection; it can keep a woman's vagina muscles so tight that intercourse is nearly impossible. Guilt caused by previous sexual experiences can have the same effect.

LOVE ... "TILL DEATH DO US PART"

"Love is patient

Eager though we may be to have needs met and dreams fulfilled, we do not demand instant satisfaction to all our desires. We remind ourselves that a relationship that does not continue to grow is dying. Ours will grow—because our marriage is worth our energy and attention.

and kind;

We will always listen to each other. We will call on God's power to work within us as we try to understand and meet the other's needs.

it is not jealous

Daily, we'll tell and show each other "you are the most important person in my life." Secure in the other's love, we will not allow lesser relationships to threaten us.

or conceited or proud;

Because we recognize that all talents and successes are gifts from God, neither of us needs to "win," to be the most important one in the world's eyes.

love is not ill-mannered

We will give each other the same politeness, consideration, and attention we give to a most honored guest.

or selfish

For each of us, the other's needs will be as important as our own.

or irritable;

Recognizing that irritability is often caused by suppressed anger or worry, we will try to be open with each other about how we really feel. Because we care about each other, we will control words and actions that might hurt the other.

love does not keep a record of wrongs;	Sometimes we will fail; sometimes we will hurt each other. But as forgiven sinners we can forgive those wrongs without getting even and without keeping score.
love is not happy with evil, but is happy with the truth.	Because Christ lives in us, we can encourage each other to study His word and live in His light.
Love never gives up; and its faith, hope, and patience never fail.	We give total, lifelong commitment to this marriage and to each other. Even if bad times come, we will not give up; we will struggle and pray and love and grow.
Love is eternal."	We are one in Christ—forever.
1 Corinthians 13:4-8 TEV	

WHY DOES A PIECE OF PAPER—A MARRIAGE CERTIFICATE—MAKE A DIFFERENCE?

The marriage certificate is a public commitment to make the relationship work, "for better or for worse." You say to each other, "No matter what happens—I will be there. If a child is conceived, we accept responsibility for that child—together."

Some people are afraid of marriage since it means total commitment and total vulnerability. If you choose unwisely, you will be badly hurt. But if both partners hold back a little, afraid to risk too much of themselves, complete intimacy will not happen—emotionally or sexually.

God intends that a man and a woman will "become one flesh" (Genesis 2:24 RSV) in marriage. This God-given oneness in sexual intercourse does not necessarily happen overnight. Sometimes years of loving communication and continual adjustment are needed to reach a completely satisfying sexual relationship.

Outside the security of a lifetime commitment, any problem triggers anxiety—and the anxiety itself can be a barrier to sexual performance.

HOW OFTEN DOES A YOUNG MARRIED COUPLE HAVE INTERCOURSE?

There are such wide differences between individuals that it is impossible to come up with a definition of what is a normal sex drive.

Even for the same person, sexual desire will vary. Much depends on how one feels on a given day. As years go by, "urgent physical needs" often give way to the desire for a more complete but less frequent, emotional and physical experience. On the other hand, a woman's sex drive may be stronger when she is in her 30s and 40s. Most men and women are physically capable of sexual activity until death.

BUILDING A GOOD MARRIAGE

So many marriages are unhappy. How can we make ours a good one?

Build your marriage on Christ; then it will not crumble when trouble comes. Jesus promised that "where two or three come together in My name, I am there with them" (Matthew 18:20 TEV). Of course, this is true in any group of Christians, but think of the power His promise adds to the intimate relationship of marriage! God works in and through each partner, helping each to find the true meaning of love, "that your joy may be complete" (John 15:11 TEV).

St. Paul compares Christian marriage to Christ's relationship with us, His church (Ephesians 5:21-33). Christ's love is the model for the love we are to have toward our mate: love that gives itself away, love that does not depend on the other *doing* anything or *being* anything, love that is totally without strings, love that does not have to be *earned* in any way.

Of course Christians, like anyone else, are affected by the times in which they live. Old-fashioned marriages were far less likely to end in divorce than marriages today. Each person had clearly spelled-out duties, and neither expected more than a reasonable amount of comfort and security.

People today expect marriage to be a loving, deeply intimate joining of two equal partners. That's much more demanding than the old-style marriage. The partners must work together to set realistic goals for themselves:

79

*When will we have children? How many? How will we
care for them? How will we handle our money? How will
we decide what we can afford? What if we disagree?*

*How will we divide household tasks? Will we do it the
way our parents did or develop our own patterns?*

*Where will we live? Will we both have careers? How will
we share in leisure activities? What material things
(house, cars, etc.) do we want? How will we make sure we
make God a part of our home? What will we do to serve
and praise Him?*

Once you have chosen your goals, you will need to decide
which ones are most important. Some goals probably must be
sacrificed or postponed to make others possible. When you
decide to have children, you will have to look also at what the
commitment to being a parent means for each of you.

Once decisions are made, the solutions are not necessarily
permanent. Children have different needs at different stages.
People change. Situations change.

Submit yourselves to one another
because of your reverence
for Christ.
Ephesians 5:21 TEV

Chapter 8
When Two Become Three

BECOMING PARENTS

When is the best time to start a family?

For one child, you must be ready for a 24-hour-a-day, 18-year commitment. If you want several children, more years are involved. They can be very good years if you are physically, emotionally, and financially ready for each child. Do not plan on your parents or anyone else taking part of the responsibility for your child—such arrangements often fall apart after a short time. There is a difference between paying for child care (even if you pay a relative, you are still responsible) and depending on someone else for help (making them responsible.)

Children are delightful, loving, cuddly charmers. They also whine, have nightmares, fight with each other, and test your

81

patience to the hilt. Since children are immature, it is important that parents themselves be mature. God both blesses us and teaches us through our children. As we respond to our children's needs, we find we can be wiser, more patient, more unselfish than we would have thought possible.

The best time to have children is when you are secure in your relationship as husband and wife and have thoroughly worked through the financial, emotional, and spiritual commitment necessary to be both a good marriage partner and a good parent.

Having a child to give a gift to your partner or to strengthen a shaky marriage is the wrong reason and can cause many problems for you, your partner, and your child.

How can a woman tell whether she's pregnant?

Doctors look for an increase in the size of the uterus and the breasts. The cervix may be softer and may have a bluish tint. They also test the blood or the urine for a hormonal change that can be detected about 10 days after conception.

The woman may have noticed any or all of these symptoms: a missed period, breast fullness and tenderness, prebreakfast nausea, unusual tiredness, frequency of urination. However, all these symptoms may have other causes. It is possible (but unusual) for a pregnant woman to have a normal period.

While home pregnancy tests are readily available today, their accuracy rate is only about 80%. Since early diagnosis of pregnancy is very important, it is far better to see a physician. There are many substances—medicines, cigarette smoke, alcohol, drugs— that can severely damage the developing fetus. Pregnant mothers who are in top-notch physical condition have much healthier babies and are less likely to have problems themselves.

Why are some couples unable to have a child?

In many cases the causes of infertility are unknown. Some people delay childbearing until their thirties or forties, decreasing somewhat their chances of conceiving a child. There are a number of diseases and infections that can damage the reproductive organs. However, the 10% of couples who fail to conceive within the first two years of unprotected intercourse have a better chance than ever before of achieving conception. If they seek treatment, about half of this 10% will succeed in conceiving.

What happens after the egg and the sperm meet in the fallopian tube?

The fertilized egg fastens itself to the cushiony wall of the uterus. A thin, tough bag forms around the egg. It is filled with a watery liquid called *amniotic fluid*. The developing baby (called an *embryo* at this stage) floats in the liquid, which protects it from bumps or changes in temperature.

At the end of two months, the embryo has a brain, eyes, ears, heart, liver, arms, legs—not fully developed yet but recognizable. After the 8th week, the embryo is called a *fetus*. By this time, a flat network of blood vessels, the *placenta*, has formed on the uterus wall. Mother and fetus have separate bloodstreams. The placenta is close to the mother's blood vessels so that food and oxygen can filter through it to the *umbilical cord* and on to the fetus. Waste materials take the same route back to the mother's bloodstream.

During the third and fourth months, nails begin to form on fingers and toes. Sex organs develop. At about 4½ months the doctor can hear the baby's heartbeat with a stethoscope. This is possible presently at 2½ months using an electronic monitor or doplar, in physicians' offices. The mother has the thrilling experience of feeling a little flutter inside her as the baby moves.

As the fetus continues to grow, the mother's uterus and abdomen stretch to many times their original size. She becomes more and more conscious of the baby moving inside her.

What causes birth defects?

Some defects are inherited; others are caused by outside factors like drugs, infection, VD, radiation, or pollutants. The risks are greater for pregnant women under 18 or over 35. Early diagnosis of pregnancy is important because commonly prescribed medicines may be harmful to a developing fetus. Accutane, an extremely effective acne medication, can cause serious birth defects if used by a pregnant woman.

Women who have what is called Rh-negative blood cells also risk birth defects in their *second* pregnancy. If the fetus has Rh-positive blood, the mother's body will attack the fetus's red blood cells. This can be prevented by vaccination after the birth of a first baby (or after a miscarriage).

Everyone should have a complete physical examination

before marriage. For women, the exam should include blood tests to check immunity to rubella and to find out blood type. Babies born to mothers who have rubella (German measles) during pregnancy often have serious birth defects. Doctors recommend that girls be vaccinated against rubella long before they conceive a child. A woman should not become pregnant until at least three months after vaccination.

What is a premature baby?

Some babies are born before the 9 months are up. If a baby is born more than a month early, she (he) will probably weigh less than 5½ pounds. Babies that small may need special care to survive. A baby weighing less than 2 pounds has only a small chance of survival, although new medical techniques now make it possible for doctors to save smaller and smaller babies.

What is a miscarriage?

Sometimes a fetus does not develop properly, so the uterus pushes it out of the body. This is called a *miscarriage* and is most likely to happen during the second or third month of pregnancy. We don't know the causes for all miscarriages, but some are due to virus infections or drugs.

How is the baby's sex decided?

All human cells, including sperm and egg cells, have 23 pairs of *chromosomes*. The chromosomes each contain many genes, different characteristics that are passed on to the next generation. About half of a man's sperm cells have a male chromosome; the other half have a female chromosome. The question of male or female depends on which sperm happens to reach the egg cell first.

What decides color of hair, musical ability, intelligence—all the things people inherit from their parents?

People inherit possibilities from their parents—hair that will be shiny black if clean and healthy, intelligence and musical ability that may or may not be developed. Most of us inherit far more natural talent than we ever use.

However, all these possibilities are in the new cell that forms when the sperm meets the egg. A woman's body makes hundreds of egg cells in her lifetime, each with a different combination of genes. Some genes carry characteristics she does not have herself, such as red hair like her great-grandfather's.

A man's body makes millions of sperm cells in his lifetime, each with a different combination of genes from his family. The baby's characteristics will depend on which sperm cell meets which egg cell. One of the special wonders of parenthood is seeing some of your own characteristics blended with those of the person you love best, creating a totally unique individual.

What happens in childbirth?

Powerful muscles in the uterus contract for 30 seconds or so, then relax. The contractions feel like a mild menstrual cramp and are about 15—20 minutes apart at first, but gradually become stronger and closer together. The uterus is slowly pushing the baby downward. At some point, the bag of amniotic fluid breaks and the liquid flows out through the vagina.

Gradually the cervix opening expands from about ⅛ inch to about 4 inches. More contractions push the baby down into the vagina. The mother contracts her abdominal muscles to create more "push"; often the father helps by holding her and/or encouraging her. Many parents-to-be attend classes that prepare them for this moment.

The baby's head usually appears first, then one shoulder followed by the other. The doctor guides and supports, but never pulls, the baby.

When the baby is breathing normally, the umbilical cord is cut about 3 inches from the abdomen. In time the stump will dry up and fall off, leaving a navel behind.

Its work finished, the placenta is now expelled from the mother's body. The entire birth process ordinarily takes about 8—20 hours for a first child.

How painful is childbirth?

Not very, for most women. Pregnant women who are well informed about what to expect tend to be more relaxed and therefore experience less pain. Many women learn exercises and breathing techniques that give them some control over the process, and they like that. But each individual is different. No one should feel she is a failure because she needed pain-killing drugs during childbirth.

Is it harder to give birth to twins or triplets?

Not really. Because she is carrying more weight around, the mother may be a little more uncomfortable during the last month or so. But the babies are born one at a time. Since they are likely to be smaller than other babies, they may need special care for a while.

What is the difference between identical twins and fraternal twins?

Fraternal twins (or triplets or whatever) are conceived when two different sperm cells join two different egg cells. Although they often feel especially close to each other, they each inherited a different set of characteristics from their parents.

Identical twins are conceived when one sperm cell joins one egg cell. The fertilized cell splits into two or more cells that are exactly alike, and each of these divided cells grows into a separate individual. Although identical twins begin life with the same set of inherited characteristics, they have different experiences and make different choices. Each becomes a unique individual, exactly like no one else in the world. Each has her (his) own special relationship with God.

If children are a gift from God, why are so many young parents tired and depressed?

All new parents get tired, since the new member of the family is quite apt to sleep all day and howl all night. Caring for a new baby is a *lot* of work, especially during the first month or two. Normal hormonal changes in a new mother's body can also cause depression. Some mothers who quit jobs for parenting find it hard to get used to being at home. Some find it helpful to take one college course, do volunteer work—anything that adds some mental stimulation and adult companionship to their lives.

New parents can become upset because they don't measure up to their own ideals of what a good parent should be and do. They can't always soothe the baby when she (he) is crying. Perhaps the mother is unable to nurse the baby as she had hoped. When they stop trying to be superparents, they'll enjoy parenting more.

Sometimes new parents need professional guidance as they struggle to adjust. If you know a parent who feels anger and rejection most of the time, urge her (him) to see a pastor or contact Family Service or the local Mental Health Association. Parents who desert or abuse their children are usually people who cannot cope and do not ask for help.

Even normal parents sometimes have mixed feelings about their baby. They love and yet sometimes they don't like him (her) very much. They may resent the changes the baby has brought to their lives or feel trapped, weighed down by responsibility. If they give each other love, understanding, and support, this shared experience will end up being a very positive one. Talking about feelings helps. So does prayer. As time goes on, the new parents will find that, although feelings of irritation and anger come and go, their love for their child is a basic, growing part of their love for each other and for God.

BIRTH CONTROL

Unfortunately, the terms "birth control" and "contraception" are often used as if they meant one and the same thing.

Strictly speaking, "birth control" refers to anything that controls/prevents a birth. Thus it includes abortion—destroying a fertilized egg or embryo or fetus. Because abortion ends a human life, it is clearly contrary to God's Word—and thus is unacceptable as a "birth control" method.

But the common understanding of the term "birth control" refers to methods for *preventing* the union of sperm cell and egg cell. These methods of *contraception* (which prevent conception) do *not* end a human life. (The intrauterine device [IUD] and the morning-after-pill are *not* true contraceptives since they do not prevent the male sperm from joining or fertilizing the female ovum. Rather, they prevent a fertilized ovum from being implanted in the uterus and continuing its development and are actually abortive in character. Apart from this consideration, the medical profession acknowledges certain risks associated with the IUD and the morning-after-pill. An early IUD, the Dalkon Shield, caused serious side effects.)

BIRTH CONTROL METHODS (CONTRACEPTION)

What is the best method of birth control?

There is no one method that is best for everyone. A doctor can help a married couple decide on a method that will work well for them and is compatible with their religious beliefs. Since effectiveness depends on proper use, the method must be acceptable to both partners. It's best if both share the responsibility of remembering the doctor's instructions and following them exactly.

Birth Control Pills

What are they?
A series of pills that make it unlikely that a woman's ovaries will release an egg cell. They also prevent a fertilized cell from attaching to the uterus wall. To be effective, the pills must be prescribed by a doctor and must be taken on schedule. A yearly physical exam is important.

Advantages?
Convenient to use. Very effective.

Disadvantages?
Many women have unpleasant side effects that may include nausea, weight gain, irregular or painful menstrual flow, sore breasts, rash, headaches, intolerance of contact lenses, depression, or nervousness. For a few users there are serious side effects including high blood pressure, heart attacks, strokes, blood clots, and gall bladder disease. The greatest risks are run by women who smoke heavily, have any undiagnosed uterine or vaginal bleeding, or a history of heart or liver disease. There is also an increased risk for women who are still growing or who are over 35.

Reliability?
Out of 100 women, less than 1 will become pregnant in 1 year.

Spermicidal Chemicals

What are they?

Spermicidal chemicals destroy sperm and block sperm from entering the cervix. They are available at drugstores without a prescription. The most effective form of spermicide is aerosol foam, which is placed high into the vagina with a plastic applicator. Spermicidal creams and gels are effective when used with a condom or diaphragm. The suppository form, a melt-away solid, is the least effective. The suppository must melt before it forms a barrier to the cervix; the time required for melting can vary considerably from one woman to another.

Advantages?

Other than occasional allergies, no side effects have been noted so far.

Disadvantages?

There is a higher risk of user failure with this method than with most other methods. This method works best when both partners are willing to share contraceptive responsibility; they must work together to read the directions carefully and follow them precisely.

Reliability?

Out of 100 women, 5 will become pregnant in a year if foam is used according to directions. Because of human error, up to 40% of women using this method will actually become pregnant.

Diaphragm with Spermicide

What is it?

A thin, shallow rubber cap on a ring. It fits over the cervix, the opening to the uterus. Always used with a spermicidal jelly. If any sperm cells slip past the diaphragm, they are stopped by the jelly. Must be prescribed by a doctor.

Advantages?

No serious side effects. A few women experience allergic reactions or more frequent urinary tract infections.

Disadvantages?

Some people might not bother using it every time. Some find

it messy and inconvenient. The doctor must be careful to prescribe the correct size and give thorough instructions for use. The diaphragm must be inspected regularly for breaks or tears; it should be replaced annually.

Reliability?

Out of 100 women, 3 will become pregnant in 1 year (when diaphragm is used properly). Out of 100 who try to use a diaphragm, 12 will become pregnant. Most failures happen during the first six months of use.

Condom

What is it?

A thin rubber sheath that covers the penis during intercourse and catches the semen. Can be bought in a drugstore without a doctor's prescription.

Advantages?

The only birth control method that offers some protection against VD.

Disadvantages?

Care is needed to prevent the condom from tearing or coming off. Some men say it dulls the pleasure of intercourse. Most effective when used with spermicide.

Reliability?

Out of 100 women, 3 will become pregnant in 1 year if condom is used according to package instructions. In actual use 5–10 will become pregnant. When condom is combined with contraceptive foam, 1 out of 100 women will become pregnant when directions are followed. In actual use of this combination, estimates are that up to 5% will become pregnant.

Contraceptive Sponge

What is it?

A soft, round, form-like sponge that has been treated with a spermicide. The sponge is moistened with tap water and then inserted high into the vagina. It has a ribbon-like loop for easy removal. The sponge may be purchased in a drugstore without a doctor's prescription.

Advantages
Fairly easy to insert; not messy; disposable; safer than birth control pills.

Disadvantages
If the sponge is incorrectly inserted, it may be difficult to remove. Some women experience an allergic reaction to spermicide. A small number of toxic shock syndrome cases have been reported among contraceptive sponge users, but no connection has been proven.

Reliability?
Out of 100 women, 9 to 27 will become pregnant within 1 year. For women who had never borne a child, the rate was 12.5 within 1 year.

Natural Family Planning

What is it?
Conception happens only if intercourse takes place just before or just after an egg cell is released by an ovary—about 7 days a month. If the woman can figure out when her "unsafe" period is, she does not have intercourse during that time. She takes her temperature every morning (it rises when the egg is released) and/or checks changes in her normal vaginal discharges. The older method of keeping a menstrual calendar (rhythm method) is less effective.

Advantages?
Some people prefer a natural method for religious or other reasons. No side effects. Helpful in planning a desired pregnancy.

Disadvantages?
Fertility awareness methods are confusing and difficult for many people. Many who try these methods become careless and discouraged. Both husband and wife need to have a serious

91

commitment to making it work. They usually need considerable advice and support from a doctor or counselor.

Reliability?

Temperature Method: Out of 100 women who follow directions exactly, 7 will become pregnant in 1 year. Because of human error, 20 will actually become pregnant in 1 year.

Vaginal Discharge Method: Out of 100 women who follow directions exactly, 2 will become pregnant in 1 year. Out of 100 who try to use this method, 25 will become pregnant in 1 year.

Sterilization

What is it?

In women, the fallopian tubes are cut so the egg and sperm cells cannot meet. In men, the vas deferens is cut so that sperm cannot mix with the semen. For both women and men, sterilization does not interfere with any sexual process other than the ability to conceive new life. Women continue to menstruate; men continue to ejaculate.

Advantages?

Freedom from further birth control measures and from the fear of pregnancy often adds to sexual pleasure.

Disadvantages?

If a person changes his (her) mind, reversing the operation is difficult—often impossible.

Reliability?

Out of 100 women or men (only one partner need be sterilized), there will be less than 1 pregnancy in 1 year.

Note: All statistics taken from *Contraceptive Technology,* 1980—81.

Chapter 9
Tough Questions

What actually happens in an abortion?
How can a sexy magazine or an R-rated movie possibly hurt me?
How can I protect myself against rape?
Why do promiscuous people act the way they do?
What causes homosexuality?

Most of this chapter zeros in on questions you have probably thought about at one time or another. The questions cover a wide range of topics.

Can sperm swim through jeans?

Not if they're on. Social workers who operate a telephone question-answering service report that this is the most common question asked by teen callers. It is very unusual for a woman to get pregnant without sexual intercourse. However, it is a

93

possible result of heavy petting. If sperm are deposited on the vulva, they may travel into the vagina and on through to the uterus to a fallopian tube.

Many unwanted pregnancies have begun when people had sexual intercourse in what they've been told is a "safe" way or when they use birth control methods incorrectly. Pregnancy *can* happen
—the first time a person has intercourse
—after intercourse in *any* position
—on *any* day of a woman's menstrual cycle
—even though the woman does not come to orgasm

A woman *cannot* prevent pregnancy by
—taking a birth control pill that morning
—jumping up and down after intercourse
—putting a tampon in the vagina first
—douching (washing out the vagina) with cola or anything else (can cause an infection)
—drinking ice water after intercourse to "freeze her organs"

A man *cannot* prevent pregnancy by
—using plastic wrap or a plastic bag to catch the semen
—withdrawing his penis just before ejaculating.
This method sometimes works but is very unreliable.
Sperm can leave the penis before ejaculation.

I'm not married, and I think I am pregnant. What should I do? Where can I go for help? I CAN'T tell my parents.

Right now you are probably feeling panicky—guilty—worried sick. Maybe you think you have destroyed your relationship with your parents—or even your relationship with God. Are you wondering whether your parents will ever forgive you? Will God forgive you?

God will. Talk to Him about what you have done and how you feel. Jesus didn't even scold the woman caught in the act of adultery. Instead, He protected her from those who would harm her and sent her home with the words "Do not sin again" (John 8:1-13 TEV).

Jesus will forgive both you and the baby's father—and gladly welcome you back. Remember the Lost Sheep (Luke 15:1-7). Jesus will stick by you in the difficult months ahead.

Remember too that God works through other people—your parents, for instance.

If you feel unable to talk to your parents right now, some other possibilities are:

a pastor or church youth worker,
a school counselor or school nurse,
your family doctor or a doctor at a clinic.

Professional ethics—and, often, state laws—forbid any of the professionals listed above from telling your parents without your consent. However, whoever you talk to will probably urge you to confide in your parents without delay, for the following reasons:

Your parents are likely to be more supportive, more helpful, more forgiving, than you think. Yes, they will be angry and hurt at first. But they will be even more hurt when they find out later that you have shut them out of this crisis in your life.

They are almost certain to find out sooner or later. Even now, they are probably uneasily aware that something is wrong. When you lie to someone you love, you move further and further away from them. The secret makes a wall between you and people who probably love you very deeply.

You have some decisions to make that will profoundly affect the lives of several people, including the baby's father and your unborn child. You need help in exploring the consequences of each option open to you.

Even more important, you need to think through the moral issues involved so that someday you will look back and say, "I made the right choice." Even though your parents may be too emotionally upset to guide you, they can help you find the kind of Christian counseling you need.

A caring, professionally trained and Christian counselor can also help you, your parents, and your boyfriend understand each other better. Even when parents try hard to forgive and understand, they can't easily get rid of their feelings of anger, disappointment, and failure. This will be a very painful time for all of you, and you need all the support you can get.

95

My friend Mollie knows for sure she is pregnant. She says she wants to keep her baby. Is that a good idea?

That depends. Single parent families can work if the parent is well prepared for the responsibility of a child. Enough money, enough maturity, enough emotional and physical strength—all these are essential.

Some unwed mothers look forward very much to having a baby to love. "The baby will always love me," they figure. "I'd much rather take care of a baby than go to school!"

But the baby is much more work than school ever was. The longed-for love grows slowly and depends on the care and attention she is able to give the baby. There's never enough money. Jobs are scarce without a good education, but going back to school is tough to arrange when baby-sitting arrangements must be made.

Mollie could find herself trapped, permanently stuck with a monotonous and unfree life-style. And her child would suffer most of all.

Newspaper columnists like Ann Landers often print pathetic letters from young people who must deal with the problem of a much-too-early pregnancy.

Mollie and her boyfriend might decide to get married. Then the baby will have two parents.

Not necessarily. The odds are greater than 2 to 1 that the marriage will end in divorce.

Even if the marriage lasts, the chances of a happy relationship are slim—and both are likely to unconsciously blame the baby. Parents who feel their lives have been stunted by the responsibility of a child find it very difficult to meet that child's needs.

Should Mollie give her baby up for adoption?

Only Mollie can decide that. She must compare the love and care she is able to give her child with what adopted parents can give. Mollie's own feelings, and those of the child's father, must also be considered.

These days, many unwed mothers decide to keep their babies. If there are several unwed mothers in a school, they are likely to encourage each other to make the same choice they did. If Mollie decides to give up her baby, she may be making an unpopular decision, but one that will bring joy to a couple who may have been waiting for years for a baby. Church-affiliated adoption agencies have long been placing babies into Christian homes. However, it is certainly true that none of the options available to Mollie is without pain.

What about abortion? I hear there's nothing to it these days.

What you've heard is only partly true. Medically speaking, abortion is a simple procedure if done within the first three months of pregnancy. In many states, free or low-cost clinics make it possible for teens to get abortions without the consent or knowledge of their parents.

In other words, Mollie is free to make an irreversible decision without the support of people who love her very much. Although abortion may seem the easiest way out of Mollie's dilemma, it is not. Killing an embryo or fetus is not like having an infected tooth pulled. Mollie is dealing with a living being, created by God just as she herself was created by God. Even those who don't care about the judgment of God's Word may experience guilt and grief and psychological and emotional scars that take a long time to heal.

What actually happens in an abortion?

In early pregnancy, the most common method is *vacuum aspiration*. A plastic tube is inserted into the uterus. The embryo and menstrual fluids are vacuumed out. In the *D & C* method a sharp spoonshaped instrument scrapes away pieces of the embryo until it is all gone. *Saline abortion* is often used after the first three months of pregnancy. A needle inserted into the uterus draws out some amniotic fluid. This fluid is replaced with a saline (salt) solution that kills the fetus. Within 24 hours the dead fetus is expelled from the mother's body.

What does the Bible say about abortion?

The Bible says that each of us has a special relationship with God that began *before we were born.* Jeremiah writes:

> The Lord said to me, "I chose you before I gave you life, and before you were born I selected you to be a prophet to the nations." Jeremiah 1:4-5 TEV

David, the psalm writer and king, is even more specific:

> You created every part of me; You put me together in my mother's womb. . . .
>
> When my bones were being formed . . . when I was growing there in secret, You knew that I was there—You saw me before I was born.
>
> The days allotted to me had all been recorded in Your book, before any of them began. Psalm 139:13-16 TEV

The Bible also emphasizes the value of each human life. "Thou shalt not kill" is one of the Ten Commandments that God wrote with His own hand and gave in a special way to His people (Exodus 20).

There is therefore no way to justify killing a human embryo or fetus—even though some claim an abortion is justified if it saves the mother (and father) from embarrassment, broken plans for the future, or emotional pain. Life is so special that God sent His own Son to be born of a young human mother for the benefit of the whole world.

What is pornography?

Some of the most beautiful statues or pictures portray the naked human body. They give us an appreciation for how wonderfully God has made us. Unfortunately, humans take this beauty and distort it; all too often we make ourselves less than we are intended to be.

If, when you look at a picture (or whatever), you can easily remember that the picture shows a special person who is valued by God—this is not pornography. Pornography happens when a human is displayed as a sex object, a thing to be used for "kicks" for someone else's pleasure. Pornography makes us feel dirty, uneasily guilty about our sexuality, instead of proud and grateful that God has made us male or female.

Is it really wrong to just look? How can a magazine or a movie hurt me?

Where did your Christian attitudes, opinions, and values

come from? You weren't born with them. Indeed, God's Word reminds us that we all have an inborn leaning toward sin. (See, for example, Ephesians 2:3 and 4:22.) On the basis of the Bible we call this "our old sinful flesh." We know, too, from God's Word that the devil seeks to work through the "world"—the evil influences all about us—to lead God's people to sin and lack of trust in God.

By baptism God made us His own children—forgiven people who by the power of the "new man" are called to resist the devil and the sinful world.

The question then is: Is pornography part of the "world," which appeals to our sinful flesh? Or is it part of God's good creation, which appeals to our new nature and builds our spiritual life?

Pornography, in other words, can pollute our minds in the same way sewage pollutes a river.

What's wrong with R-rated movies? What if the movie is just frank and open, not dirty?

The best way to tell whether a movie is harmful is to notice the effect on your thinking. Does the movie picture a world in which God exists? Does it substitute a slick "get all you can" philosophy for honest love? Does it tear down or build Christian values?

Sometimes "frank" language has a slightly different meaning from the more polite words. Constant use of street words for sex can make intercourse seem a hostile act instead of a way to express committed love.

We can decide whether to eat roast beef or garbage. We also have the power by God's Spirit to choose what goes into our heads and hearts.

Right. It's MY head, MY body. If I happen to get a kick out of a mildly dirty magazine, that's MY business.

God has not given you absolute ownership of your body. *Don't you know that your body is the temple of the Holy Spirit, who lives in you and who was given to you by God? You do not belong to yourselves but to God; He bought you for a price. So use your bodies for God's glory.* 1 Corinthians 6:19-20 TEV

What is a flasher? Is he dangerous?

Flasher is a slang word for an exhibitionist, a person who gets sexual satisfaction from showing his (her) genitals to others. The typical flasher is a man who delights in shocking young girls. Most remain at a safe distance. They should be reported to the police so they can receive psychiatric help.

What if a woman is raped?

Rape happens when one person forces another to have sexual intercourse. Women and girls are usually the victims, although there are cases in which a homosexual man rapes another man. Most psychologists feel that rape is a crime of violence, that a rapist wants to hurt and frighten a woman rather than get sexual pleasure.

A woman who has been raped should go *immediately* to a hospital or a rape crisis center. A doctor will check her for injuries and will also look for sperm cells in the vagina, evidence that the rape really happened. (No police report will be made without her consent. But if she delays or washes herself first, it may not be possible to prove anything.) The doctor also takes steps to prevent venereal disease.

The doctor can also recommend agencies that will provide free or inexpensive counseling. Most victims need spiritual and emotional support as well as medical attention. A woman should seek help from her pastor or somebody she trusts as a committed Christian to receive the support in Christ that she needs.

How can a woman protect herself?

Many women believe that nothing can ever happen to them. They take chances that are foolish. But the best way to protect yourself is to stay away from dangerous situations, like hitch-hiking or walking alone at night. It's important to be alert so you will recognize danger when you see it. This true story illustrates why:

It was dusk when Karen and her friends got to the football game. They were hardly inside the gate when she decided she wanted the jacket she had left in the car. She hurried back to the parking lot, slipped on her jacket, and headed back to the stadium. "Hi, Karen!" called one of a little group of guys in the darker area next to the lot. "Come here a minute!" Karen was in the middle of the group before she realized she didn't know any of them. They must have heard her name when she first walked through the lot with her friends.

The biggest guy held a knife against Karen's ribs. Another grabbed her arm. They were walking her toward their car when another car distracted their attention. Karen wrenched her arm out of the guy's grasp and ran, leaving him holding her jacket. She never got the jacket back, and the young men were never caught, but she was safe!

What is incest?

Incest is having sexual relations with a member of your family or another close relative. It is a crime. Because of the prohibitions against incest, it is against the law to marry someone in one's immediate family, like a brother or sister or father or mother. In many places first cousins are not allowed to marry.

Incest is more common than most people think. It happens in all kinds of families—rich and poor, white and black, churchgoing and nonreligious.

Usually, an older person will convince a younger or weaker person that this twisted form of sex is "OK" or that any guilt belongs to the younger person for being "such a tease." This is a betrayal of trust and is *never* true. The victim is *not* guilty and will probably suffer severe spiritual and psychological damage if the relationship continues.

She (he) should firmly resist any future advances, and should talk over the problem with a parent or pastor or other trusted counselor. The victim of incest needs help. And so does the aggressor.

What is a prostitute?

A prostitute is a person who engages in sexual activity for money. Most prostitutes are women; most customers are men.

Both the number of prostitutes in the U.S. and Canada and the number of cutomers have dropped steadily in recent years. Because of pressure from churches and women's rights advocates, many police vice squads now arrest (and publicize names of) customers as well as the prostitutes themselves.

Why do promiscuous people act the way they do?

A *promiscuous* person has sexual intercourse with many different partners. Although a promiscuous woman is usually looked down on in our culture, a promiscuous man may be envied by some. However, researchers find very little difference in the personality and family backgrounds of these men and women. Their sex drive is no stronger than anyone else's, but they have a great need for something that will blot out their emotional problems.

Promiscuous people usually have very little self-confidence, accept little responsibility for their own behavior, and blame others for their own shortcomings. Because they do not take the time and effort to build a lasting relationship, they never discover how wonderful sex can be. Most sad of all, they are substituting sinful "thrills" for something much more thrilling: a close relationship with Jesus Christ.

Is a nymphomaniac a promiscuous woman?

Not exactly. A true nymphomaniac is a very sick woman. Her uncontrollable sexual desires cause her to seek sexual intercourse with anyone, at any cost. This mental illness is very rare.

Marriage counselors and psychologists report that most cases of alleged nymphomania turn out to be perfectly normal women. Sometimes husband and wife feel unable to talk to each other about their sexual relationship. The wife may be accused of being a nymphomaniac because at this time in her life she has a stronger sex drive than her husband does. Although they both are normal, they feel threatened because no woman is "supposed to" want to have sexual intercourse more than her husband does. Once the incorrect diagnosis is out of the way, the counselor is usually able to help them work things out.

What are sadism and masochism?

In both, sex is linked with violence, twisting God's good gift into something vile and nasty. Either physical or psychological pain is made part of the sex act. A sadist likes to give pain; a masochist either wants pain or is willing to suffer anything to please the partner.

People who believe that sex is shameful and dirty are most vulnerable to this mental disorder. Some psychologists blame an increase in the numbers of sadists and masochists on the common approval of aggressiveness and even violence in our society. For instance, movies and TV shows often glorify violence and combine it with sex.

What is fetishism?

Nearly everyone finds certain things more sexually exciting than others. We may be aroused by a particular part of the body (hair, breasts), by an article of clothing, or (if you can believe the ads) by a certain perfume. For a fetishist (usually male), this preference turns into a compulsion. One particular object, often a piece of clothing, becomes "the loved one" for him and takes the place of a sex partner in his life. He will steal or even hurt someone in order to get it.

Another form of fetishism is *kleptomania*, compulsive stealing. Here the sick person is usually a woman who feels unloved and unwanted. She steals objects that have no value to her, other than the sexual excitement she gets from the act of stealing and from the object itself.

In *pyromania*, the fetishist has a compulsive desire for fire. He gets sexual excitement from setting fires and watching them burn.

What is the difference between a transvestite and a trans-sexual? Are they homosexuals?

No. A *transvestite* is a person (usually male) who enjoys dressing in clothes of the opposite sex. Some habitually wear one item, like a bra or panties, under their own clothing. Others dress completely in women's clothing, either once in a while or—in extreme cases—all the time.

Most transvestites have normal sexual relationships with women. They marry and father children. They want only to be left alone to indulge in their desire to wear female clothing.

Transsexuals see themselves as the opposite sex; they feel trapped in the wrong body. They see the sex organs they were born with as deformities.

A typical transsexual is a man who wants to live the life of a woman. He wants a heterosexual relationship with another man but is not interested in homosexual men.

Some doctors now treat transsexuals with hormones. Sex-change surgery is another option, now less common because too many operations were unsuccessful. Since either treatment is quite drastic, doctors study potential patients very carefully before accepting them. In spite of the number of transsexuals you may have seen on talk shows, this is a very rare condition.

What about homosexuality?

Homosexuals are persons who are sexually attracted to those of their own sex. Some homosexual pairs express these desires by caressing each other to orgasm.

Researchers disagree about the number of homosexuals in North America today. Although "gays" have become less secretive about their sexual orientation, no one knows how many still conceal their true sex preference.

The person who is sexually attracted to both sexes is called a bisexual.

Some experts believe homosexuality is an inborn characteristic like blue eyes or a big nose. Another theory suggests that it is the result of sex hormones that are out of balance.

Other researchers believe that homosexual attitudes may be formed when a young child lacks a loving relationship with the parent of the same sex. Although most psychologists think sexual preferences are set long before puberty, some feel that repeated, cruel rejection by the opposite sex may lead a young teen to look for warmth and acceptance in members of his (her) own sex.

Psychologists who believe an unloving father may cause a boy to develop homosexual attitudes also point out that this kind of environment does not have that effect on everyone. Most boys who did not have a father's love turn out to be heterosexual (straight) men. Most girls who have unpleasant experiences with males turn out to be heterosexual women. So the cause of homosexuality remains a mystery.

What does the Bible say about homosexuality?

The Bible description of sexual love within marriage, "the two shall become one," clearly refers to a relationship between a man and a woman. Romans 1:27 says that homosexual behavior is one of the results of sinfulness. Nowhere in the Bible is there any approval for homosexuality as an "alternate life-style."

While we as Christians cannot therefore condone homosexual behavior, we will want to show concern for the homosexual person. We will proclaim also to the homosexual that God forgives sin for Christ's sake and makes possible a new life through the power of the Holy Spirit.

Sometimes a slightly built boy or a husky girl is labeled "homosexual" simply because of appearance and/or interests that may be different from the average. Such a wrongly applied label can follow a person for years and influence the way that person is treated by others. As Christians we surely will avoid such name-calling, gossip, or labeling, which can seriously injure another person. The fact is that most homosexuals look and act just like everyone else.

Can a person change from homosexuality to heterosexuality?

Some therapists have succeeded in helping people change from homosexual to heterosexual behavior. The therapy works only if the homosexual person has a strong desire to change.

How can I be sure I am not a homosexual?

Many young people worry unnecessarily about homosexual tendencies they suspect in themselves. They may have had one or more experiences with somebody of the same sex in which touching or other play resulted in orgasm. These experiences do not mean that someone is a homosexual.

It is also normal to have a deep attachment of friendship to someone of the same sex. David and Jonathan (1 Samuel 18), for instance, had a sincere love for each other that was very different from their normal sexual interest in the women they loved.

Many young people admire teachers or others who are the same sex. It is normal to admire someone very much and want to be near that person. Often this admiration helps you discover the direction you would like your own life to take.

No one should call himself (herself) homosexual until, as an adult, he (she) notices a constant, firm sexual interest in persons of the same sex. If you are worried about this, talk to your pastor or another adult about your feelings.

It often takes a long time for a young person to feel at ease with members of the other sex. Be patient with yourself. Remember that you are not the only one who fears rejection; others feel just as insecure as you do. Ask God to help you become more comfortable with your own sexuality. He will.

Chapter 10
Scrapbook

This chapter is a scrapbook: a collection of quotes, prayers, and thought-starters. We hope you'll use them as boosters, as ways to begin talking with God about your sexuality, as reminders that you are not—and never will be—alone.

Too Far, Too Soon

I don't do the good I want to do; instead, I do the evil that I do not want to do . . . To be controlled by human nature results in death; to be controlled by the Spirit results in life and peace.

Romans 7:19; 8:6 TEV

What happens to my good intentions when I'm with her? Why does my desire for her override everything else? Because I am so much in love with her, I forget plans for the future—my parents' love for me—my own deep knowledge of right and wrong.

At least I *think* I'm in love. When we are together, I always want to be close to her. She's the kindest, most fun, prettiest girl I've ever met. Being with her is wonderful. Is that love? Will I still feel the same way five years from now?

I wonder how she feels about our growing closer together. What does she really want? I know we shouldn't go on like this, but what will she think if I back off now? Maybe we should talk over what our limits ought to be—but I wouldn't know how to begin.

God, thank You for my sexuality, for the body you have given me. But I need more! For one thing, I need Your forgiveness for so often misusing Your gifts. I need Your support, Your wisdom as I turn around and begin again. Give me the right words to talk to her about how we feel about each other.

Lord Jesus, I really do want Your Spirit to control my life. Help me remember that tonight!

In Love, I Think

Sing for joy to the Lord, all the earth; praise Him with songs and shouts of joy! Sing praises to the Lord! Play music on the harps! Blow trumpets and horns, and shout for joy to the Lord, our King.
Psalm 98:4-6 TEV

I feel like cartwheels across the lawn, like fizzy bubbles rising to the top of a glass of gingerale, like trumpets and cymbals and drums. When the Marching Band plays the victory song, it feels as if they're playing it for me.

I think—I am almost positive!—that he likes me as much as I like him. Surely two people couldn't laugh and talk and enjoy life together as we do, without both realizing that something special is happening. It's hard to believe that a few weeks ago we hardly knew each other.

So far, we haven't spoken much about serious things—yet somehow I know You mean as much to him as You do to me. The way he treats me—and the way he treats others—tells me a lot. When I see him at church, I feel sure he is there by choice.

Lord, what is this wonderful feeling? When I'm near him, my bones melt. My heart pounds. I feel dizzy. Is this truly love, or just the excitement of getting to know someone who really attracts me? Whatever it is, it's the most thrilling thing that has ever happened to me, and I don't want it to ever end.

Yes, Lord. I know You have a plan for me, much better than anything I could work out by myself. Maybe he is part of Your plan—or maybe this giddy love (?) I feel now is only for today.

Whatever happens in the future, I feel great today. The happy feeling inside me right now has to be a gift from You—thank You! Thank You, Lord Jesus, for caring about my todays and about my future. Because I am important to You, I can enjoy today, and still learn and plan and think and grow. I can leave my future in Your loving hands.

Not Good Enough

The Lord who created you says, "Do not be afraid—I will save you. I have called you by name—you are Mine."

Isaiah 43:1 TEV

The truth is, I'm a failure. Not good enough to get on the team—to have dates—to be popular—to make my parents proud of me.

Big feet. Knobby knees. A million pimples. Hair that won't act like I want it to. All the charm of a week-old baloney sandwich.

Why, Lord? Why do I always say such dumb things—if I can think of anything to say at all? Why do people ignore me, act like I'm not even there? Why am I always on the outside, watching other people have fun?

I know it's my own fault sometimes. I get so discouraged I give up before I even start. Some days I hardly speak to anyone. Other times, something inside me makes me act stupid and silly—to get their attention, I guess.

Keep telling me I am Yours, Lord Jesus. Remind me—again and again—that You love me just as I am. Since I don't like myself very much, show me how I can change. Give me opportunities to make friends. Help me appreciate the specialness You have created within me. Help me to listen when You call my name.

Decisions

Our life is a matter of faith, not of sight.

2 Corinthians 5:7 TEV

Ever since I can remember, I have longed to be grown up.

It's fun to think about having my own car—being able to stay out as long as I want—being free to travel and work and play at a pace *I* set. The really hard choices—about love and marriage and children—have seemed very remote and far away.

But lately I've met people not much older than I who have already made their choices. At 16 or 17 they have found themselves in situations that will affect *the rest of their lives.* How do I know I won't be trapped by my own mistakes?

Sometimes I think being alone is the only way to keep from being hurt. I see steady couples torn by jealousy and hurt feelings, marriages ripped apart, families who do nothing but yell at each other. Is love really worth the risk?

You think so, don't You, Jesus? You allowed Yourself to be tortured, deserted by friends, misunderstood—for love's sake. You were willing to suffer anything to make the church—all of us—your bride. I know I can always count on Your love for me, on Your unchanging presence in my life. Troubles may come, but I cling to the belief that You will show me how to love and be loved.

Although I have made many mistakes, You have taught me how to choose friends and how to be a friend. Guide me now as I learn how to be a loving person.

Not Far Enough?

This means that He had to become like His brothers in every way . . . . And now He can help those who are tempted, because He Himself was tempted and suffered.

Hebrews 2:17-18 TEV

Is there something wrong with me? Am I incomplete, Lord? Unmasculine? What do other people say about me behind my back? Do they call me queer? Or cold? Or stupid?

Does everyone else really do it? Is it as great as they claim? Am I missing something wonderful by waiting? Lord, when they joke about the girls they've been with, I don't know what to say. Usually I pretend not to understand their questions—or I kid around with them, say something they can take any way they like. Either way, I feel like a fool.

I like girls, Lord. I'm pretty sure that my sex drive is as strong as anybody's. And even though I'm careful not to let things go too far, I *want* to be free and warm and loving. And sometimes I feel very unwilling to wait any longer. I want it *now*.

What kinds of feelings did You experience, Jesus, as You were growing up? I have trouble picturing You struggling with problems and temptations like mine—yet I know You were like me in this way as in all others.

Help me, Lord, to remember You understand how I feel, so I can talk and question and confess freely to You—and get Your power to act in Your way.

GLOSSARY

Abortion (a-BOR-shun)	The premature termination of a pregnancy. There are three types: *voluntary*, a procedure performed at the request of the pregnant woman; *spontaneous* (miscarriage), a natural termination usually due to some abnormal development of the fetus; *therapeutic*, a medically recommended procedure prompted by abnormal developments that threaten the mother's life or the fetus.
Abstinence (AB-stin-ens)	To voluntarily avoid: In sexual connotation, to refrain from sexual intercourse.
Acne (AK-nee)	A condition of the complexion, characterized by pimples, blackheads, and/or excess oiliness. Common in adolescents.
Adolescence (a-doh-LES-sens)	The period of life between puberty and adulthood.
Adultery (a-DULL-ter-ee)	Sexual intercourse with a person who is legally married to someone else. The term is often used to describe any sexual intercourse outside of marriage.
AIDS	(Acquired Immune Deficiency Syndrome) A life-threatening viral disease transmitted through exchange of blood and/or semen either by sexual contact or by use of dirty needles in "shooting" drugs.
Amniocentesis (am-nee-o-sen-TEE-sis)	A procedure whereby a sample of the amniotic fluid surrounding the fetus is drawn and analyzed to detect possible birth defects.
Amnion (AM-nee-on)	The thin membrane which forms the sac of water surrounding the fetus within the uterus. Contains amniotic fluid, in which the fetus is immersed for protection against shocks and jolts.
Androgen (AN-dro-jen)	A hormone which influences growth and the sex drive in the male. Produces masculine secondary sex characteristics (voice changes, hair growth, etc.).
Anus (AY-nuss)	The opening at the base of the buttocks through which solid waste is eliminated from the intestines.
Artificial Insemination	The medical procedure of injecting semen into the vagina close to the cervix by artificial means; can enable pregnancy in spite of fertility problems.
Birth Control	See Contraception.
Bisexual (by-SECKS-shoo-al)	Having both male and female sex organs. Commonly used term to describe a sexual interest in both sexes.
Bladder (BLAD-er)	A sac in the pelvic region where urine is stored until elimination.
Breech Birth	The birth position when the baby's feet or buttocks appear first instead of the usual (headfirst) position.

Caesarean Section (si-SAIR-ee-an)	(Caesarean Birth; "C" Section) Delivery of a baby by surgical incision through the abdomen into the uterus.
Castration (kas-TRAY-shun)	Removal of the sex glands—the testicles in men, the ovaries in women.
Cervix (SER-vicks)	The narrow, lower part of the uterus, which opens into the deep portion of the vagina.
Chancre (SHANG-ker)	A small sore or ulcerated area, usually on the genitals, which is the first symptom of syphilis.
Change of Life	See Climacteric; Menopause.
Chastity (CHAS-ti-tee)	Abstention from illicit sexual intercourse.
Chlamydia (kla-MID-ee-ah)	See Venereal Disease.
Chromosome (KRO-mo-soam)	One of the more or less rodlike bodies found in the nucleus of all cells, containing the heredity factors or genes. 22 pairs of chromosomes account for a person's hereditary characteristics. The 23rd pair determines sex. See X Chromosome and Y Chromosome.
Circumcision (ser-kum-SIZH-un)	Surgical removal of the foreskin or prepuce of the penis. Originally a Jewish rite performed as a sign of reception into their faith; now generally performed for purposes of cleanliness.
Climacteric (kly-MACK-ter-ik)	The time of physical and emotional change—the end of menstruation in women and a lessening of sex-hormone production in both sexes. See Menopause and Mid-Life Crisis.
Climax	See Orgasm.
Clitoris (KLIT-or-iss)	A small, highly sensitive female organ located just above the urethra. Compares to the penis in males.
Coitus (KO-ih-tus)	Sexual intercourse between male and female, in which the penis is inserted into the vagina.
Conception (kon-SEP-shun)	(Impregnation) Penetration of the ovum (female egg cell) by a sperm, resulting in development of an embryo—new life.
Condom	See Contraception.
Congenital (kon-JEN-i-tal)	Existing from birth. May or may not be inherited.
Contraception (kon-trah-SEP-shun)	(Birth control) The prevention of conception by use of devices, drugs, or other means in sexual intercourse. Commonly used methods are: *Birth Control Pill* A contraceptive drug made of synthetic hormones which prevent ovulation. Available only on prescription and must be taken as prescribed. *Condom* (KON-dum) A thin rubber sheath placed over the erect penis before intercourse to prevent the sperm from entering the vagina.

Vaginal Foam, Jelly, Suppositories, etc. Non-prescription products for the female which are applied within the vagina. Most contain a spermicide—chemical substance which destroys sperm cells.

Diaphragm (DIE-a-fram) A thin rubber disc which covers the cervix and prevents sperm from entering the uterus. Must be individually fitted by a doctor.

Premature Withdrawal Withdrawal of the penis from the vagina before ejaculation. Largely unreliable because of possible release of sperm before ejaculation.

Rhythm Method Abstinence from intercourse during the woman's fertile days as determined by her menstrual cycle.

Copulation	See Coitus.
Cunnilingus (kun-i-LING-us)	The act of applying the mouth or tongue to the vulva, to stimulate the female.
D & C	(Dilatation & Curettage) A medical procedure in which the cervix is dilated and a spoon-shaped medical instrument called a curette is used to scrape the lining of the uterus.
Delivery	The process of giving birth.
Douche (doosh)	The cleansing of the vagina with a stream of liquid solution or water.
Ejaculation (ee-jack-yoo-LAY-shun)	The discharge of semen from the penis.
Embryo (EM-bree-oh)	The unborn in its earliest stages of development. In humans, the fertilized ovum during the first eight weeks of its growth.
Endometrium (en-doh-MEE-tree-um)	The lining of the uterus, which thickens and fills with blood in preparation for a fertilized ovum.
Epididymis (ee-pi-DID-i-miss)	The mass of tiny coils connecting the testicles with the sperm duct.
Erection (ee-RECK-shun)	The enlargement and hardening of the penis or clitoris as tissues fill with blood, usually during sexual excitement.
Erogenous Zone (ee-RAH-jen-us)	Any area of the body that is sexually sensitive or stimulating such as mouth, lips, breasts, nipples, and genitals.
Erotic (ee-RAH-tik)	Sexually stimulating.
Estrogen (ESS-tro-jen)	A hormone which affects functioning of the menstrual cycle and produces female secondary sex characteristics (breast development, widened hips, etc.).
Eunuch (YOO-nuck)	A castrated male.

Exhibitionist (ex-i-BISH-un-ist)	A person who compulsively exposes his/her sex organs in public.
Extramarital (ex-tra-MARE-i-tal)	"Outside of marriage"; often used to refer to illicit sexual intercourse, i.e., "extramarital affair."
Fallopian Tube (fa-LOW-pee-an)	The tube through which the egg passes from each ovary to the uterus.
Fellatio (fel-LAY-show)	The act of applying the mouth or tongue to the penis to stimulate the male.
Fertility	The ability to reproduce.
Fertilization	Penetration of the female ovum by a single sperm, resulting in conception.
Fetus (FEE-tuss)	The unborn child from the third month after conception until birth.
Foreplay	The beginning stage of sexual intercourse, during which partners may kiss, caress, and touch each other in order to achieve full sexual arousal.
Foreskin	The loose skin covering the tip of the penis, removed during circumcision. Also called the prepuce (PREE-puce).
Fornication (for-ni-KAY-shun)	Sexual intercourse between unmarried men and women.
Frigidity (fri-JID-i-tee)	Commonly used term for the sexual dysfunction in which a woman is unable to respond to sexual stimulation.
Gene (jean)	The carrier for hereditary traits in chromosomes.
Genital Herpes	See Venereal Disease.
Genitalia (jen-i-TAIL-ya)	(Genitals; Genital Organs) Visible reproductive or sex organs. Usually denotes vagina, vulva, and clitoris in females and the penis and testicles in males.
Gestation (jes-TAY-shun)	The period from conception to birth, approximately nine months.
Glans (glanz)	The head of the penis, exposed when the foreskin is pushed back, or after circumcision.
Gonorrhea (gon-er-EE-uh)	See Venereal Disease.
G.U. Non-Specific	See Venereal Disease.
Gynecologist (guy-na-KOLL-o-jist)	A physician who specializes in the treatment of female sexual and reproductive organs.
Heredity (her-ED-it-ee)	Traits, characteristics, or diseases transmitted from parents to children.
Hermaphrodite (her-MAF-ro-dite)	An individual born with both male and female sex organs.

115

Heterosexual (het-er-o-SECK- shoo-al)	One who is sexually attracted to or sexually active with persons of the other sex.
Homosexual (ho-mo-SECK- shoo-al)	One who is sexually attracted to or sexually active with persons of one's own sex.
Hormone (HOR-moan)	A chemical substance, produced by an endocrine gland, which has a particular effect on the function of other organs in the body.
Hymen (HIGH-men)	A thin membrane which partially closes the entrance to the vagina. Sometimes called the maidenhead.
Hysterectomy (hiss-ter-ECK-to- mee)	Surgical removal of the uterus. May include removal of one or both ovaries (oophorectomy).
Impotence (IM-po-tens)	A type of male sexual dysfunction; inability to achieve or maintain erection of the penis during sexual intercourse.
Incest (IN-sest)	Sexual intercourse between close relatives such as father and daughter, mother and son, or brother and sister.
Intercourse, *Sexual*	See Coitus.
Jock Itch	A fungus infection causing skin irritation in the genital area.
Labor	The birth stage in which the cervix gradually dilates, allowing strong contractions of the uterine muscles to push the baby through the vagina and out of the mother's body.
Lactation (lak-TAY-shun)	The production and secretion of milk by the mammary glands in the mother's breasts, following childbirth. The process continues so long as she nurses her child.
Lesbian (LEZ-be-an)	A female homosexual.
Libido	See Sex Drive.
Maidenhead	See Hymen.
Masochism (MASS-o-kizm)	Cruelty to self; receiving sexual pleasure from having pain inflicted or by being harshly dominated.
Masturbation (mass-ter-BAY- shun)	Self-stimulation of one's sex organs, often to the point of orgasm.
Menarche (me-NAR-kee)	The onset of the menstrual cycle in a girl.
Menopause (MEN-o-pawz)	(Change of Life; Climacteric) The end of menstruation in women, usually between the ages of 45 and 55.

116

Menstruation (men-stroo-AY-shun)	The discharge through the vagina of blood from the uterus. This menstrual "period" usually occurs every 28—30 days in females, between puberty and menopause.
Midlife Crisis	Current term for the change of life (climacteric) in men, usually between ages 50 and 60; sometimes called male menopause. May evoke feelings of restlessness and failure.
Miscarriage	(Spontaneous Abortion) The natural expulsion of the fetus from the uterus, before it is mature enough to live, usually due to some abnormal development.
Nocturnal Emission (nok-TER-nal ee-MISH-un)	(Wet Dream) Involuntary male erection and ejaculation during sleep.
Nymphomaniac (nim-foe-MAY-nee-ack)	A female who experiences excessive sexual desire.
Obstetrician (ob-ste-TRISH-un)	A physician who specializes in the care of women during pregnancy, childbirth, and immediately thereafter.
Oral Sex	See Cunnilingus; Fellatio.
Orgasm (OR-gazm)	(Climax) The peak of excitement in sexual activity.
Ovaries (OH-va-rees)	The two female sex glands found on either side of the uterus, in which the ova (egg cells) are formed. They also produce hormones which influence female body characteristics.
Ovulation (oh-vyoo-LAY-shun)	Release of the mature (ripe) ovum from the ovary to the Fallopian tube.
Ovum (OH-vum)	(Plural: ova) Female reproductive cell (egg) found in the ovary. After fertilization by a male sperm, the human egg develops into an embryo and then a fetus.
Penis (PEE-nis)	Male sex organ through which semen is discharged and urine is passed.
Pituitary (pih-TOO-it-air-ee)	A gland at the base of the brain which controls functions of all the other ductless glands, especially sex glands, adrenals, and thyroid.
Placenta (plu-SEN-ta)	The spongelike organ that connects the fetus to the lining of the uterus by means of the umbilical cord. It serves to feed the fetus and to dispose of waste. Expelled from the uterus after the birth of a child (afterbirth).
Pornography (por-NOG-raf-ee)	Literature, motion pictures, art, or other means of expression which, without any concern for personal or moral values, intend simply to be sexually arousing.

Pregnancy *(PREG-nan-cee)*	Period from conception to birth; the condition of having a developing embryo or fetus within the female body.
Prenatal (pree-NAY-tal)	Before birth.
Progesterone *(pro-JES-ter-own)*	(Progestin) The female "pregnancy hormone" which prepares the uterus to receive the fertilized ovum.
Promiscuous (pro-MISS-kyoo-us)	Engaging in sexual intercourse with many persons; engaging in casual sexual relationships.
Prophylactic (prah-fil-LAK-tik)	A device or drug used to prevent disease, often specifically venereal disease. Common term for the condom.
Prostate (PRAH-state)	Male gland which surrounds the urethra and neck of the bladder and secretes part of the seminal fluid.
Prostitute (PRAH-sti-toot)	An individual who engages in sexual activity for money.
Puberty (PYOO-ber-tee)	The period of rapid development that marks the end of childhood; sex organs mature and produce either ovaries or sperm; the girl becomes a young woman and the boy a young man.
Pubic (PYOO-bik)	Regarding the lower part of the abdominal area, where hair grows in a triangular patch.
Rape (rayp)	Forcible sexual intercourse with a person who does not consent.
Rectum (RECK-tum)	The lower end of the large intestine, ending at the anus.
Rhythm Method	See Contraception.
Sadism (SAD-izm)	Cruelty; receiving sexual pleasure by inflicting pain on the sexual partner.
Safe Period	The interval in the menstrual cycle when the female is presumably not ovulating and therefore unable to become pregnant.
Scrotum (SKRO-tum)	The sac of skin suspended between the male's legs that contains the testicles.
Semen (SEE-men)	(Seminal Fluid; Seminal Emission) The fluid made up of sperm, secretions from the seminal vesicles, prostate and Cowper's glands, and the epididymis. Ejaculated through the penis when the male reaches orgasm.
Seminal Vesicles (SEM-i-nal VESS-i-cals)	Two storage pouches for sperm (which is produced in the testicles). Located on either side of the prostate, they are attached to and open into the sperm ducts.
Sex Drive	(Libido: li-BEE-doe) The desire for sexual activity.
Sex, Oral	See Cunnilingus; Fellatio.
Sex Organs	Commonly refers to the male penis and female vagina.

118

Sexual Dysfunction	Term used to describe problems in sexual performance.
Sexual Intercourse	See Coitus.
Smegma (SMEG-mah)	A thick accumulation of secretions under the foreskin of the penis or around the clitoris, which has an unpleasant odor.
Sodomy (SAH-dah-mee)	Any of a variety of sexual behaviors, broadly defined by law as deviant, such as sexual intercourse by humans with animals, mouth-genital contact, or anal intercourse between human beings.
Sperm	The male reproductive cell(s), produced in the testicles, having the capacity to fertilize the female ova, resulting in pregnancy.
Spermatic Duct (sper-MAT-ik)	(Vas Deferens) The tube in the male through which sperm passes from the epididymis to the seminal vesicles and urethra.
Spermatic Cord	The tube in the male by which the testicle is suspended; contains the sperm ducts, veins, and nerves.
Spermicide	See Contraception.
Spontaneous Abortion	See Miscarriage.
Sterility (ster-ILL-it-ee)	The inability to reproduce.
Sterilization (ster-ill-ih-ZAY-shun)	A procedure by which a male or female is rendered unable to produce children, but can still engage in sexual intercourse. Some of the most common surgical methods are: *Laparoscopy* (la-pa-ROS-ko-pee) Tiny incisions in the abdomen, through which the fallopian tubes are cut or cauterized. Also called "Band-Aid Sterilization." *Tubal Ligation* (TOO-bul lie-GAY-shun) The surgeon cuts and ties the ends of both fallopian tubes after making a larger incision in the abdomen or by going through the vagina. *Vasectomy* (vas-ECK-toe-mee) The male sperm-carrying duct is cut, part is removed, and the ends tied.
Syphilis	See Venereal Disease.
Testes (TES-teez)	(Testicles) The two male sex glands which produce sperm, suspended within a sac of skin between the legs.
Testosterone (tes-TOSS-ter-own)	Male sex hormone produced by the testes; causes and maintains male secondary sex characteristics (voice change, hair growth, etc.)
Transgenderist (trans-JEN-der ist)	A person who identifies very strongly with the other sex and may dress in the clothing of that sex.

119

Transsexual (trans-SEKS-shoo-al	One who feels psychologically like a member of the other sex, and is willing to undergo "sex change" surgery to achieve the outward appearance of the other sex.
Transvestite	One who has a compulsion to dress in the clothing of the other sex.
Trichomoniasis (trick-uh-muh-NY-uh-sis)	See Venereal Disease.
Umbilical Cord (uhm-BILL-ih-kal)	The cord connecting the fetus to the placenta, through which the fetus receives nourishment.
Urethra (yoo-REE-thra)	The duct through which urine passes from the bladder and is eliminated from the body.
Urologist (yoo-RAHL-i-jist)	A physician who specializes in treating urinary tract problems of both sexes, as well as the genital tract of males.
Uterus (YOO-ter-us)	(Womb: woom) The small, muscular, pear-shaped female organ in which the fetus develops; has the ability to accommodate the growing child (children).
Vagina (vuh-JY-na)	(Birth Canal) The canal in the female body between the uterus and the vulva; receives the penis during intercourse; the canal through which an infant passes at birth.
Vasectomy	See Sterilization.
Venereal Disease (ven-EAR-ee-al)	**(VD) More precise name is Sexually Transmitted Disease (STD). Any of a variety of contagious diseases contracted almost entirely by sexual intercourse. Some of the most common are AIDS, chlamydia, genital herpes, gonorrhea, trichomoniasis, and syphilis.**
Virgin (VER-jin)	A person who has never had sexual intercourse.
Vulva (VUL-va)	The female's external sex organs, including the *Labia majora* and *Labia minora*, the outer and inner folds of skin (lips) surrounding the vagina, and the clitoris.
Wasserman Test	A blood test to determine present or past infection with syphilis.
Wet Dream	See Nocturnal Emission.
Womb	See Uterus.
X Chromosome	A chromosome which determines sex, present in all female ova and in one-half of a male's sperm. If the egg is fertilized by a sperm having an X chromosome, a female will be conceived (XX).
Y Chromosome	A sex-determining chromosome present in one-half of a male's sperm. If an ovum is fertilized by a sperm with a Y chromosome, a male will be conceived (XY).